7 Stewardship Keys
THAT LEAD TO OVERFLOW

by Jason Hale

7 Stewardship Keys
That Lead to Overflow
by Jason Hale
© 2025 Jason Hale. All rights reserved.

No part of this publication may be reproduced or transmitted in any form or by any means, mechanical or electronic, including photocopying and recording, or by any information storage and retrieval system, without permission in writing from author or publisher (except by a reviewer, who may quote brief passages and/or show brief video clips in a review).

Disclaimer: The Publisher and the Author make no representations or warranties with respect to the accuracy or completeness of the contents of this work and specifically disclaim all warranties, including without limitation warranties of fitness for a particular purpose. No warranty may be created or extended by sales or promotional materials. The advice and strategies contained herein may not be suitable for every situation. This work is sold with the understanding that the Publisher is not engaged in rendering legal, accounting, or other professional services. If professional assistance is required, the services of a competent professional person should be sought. Neither the Publisher nor the Author shall be liable for damages arising herefrom. The fact that an organization or website is referred to in this work as a citation and/or a potential source of further in- formation does not mean that the Author or the Publisher endorses the information the organization or website may provide or recommendations it may make. Further, readers should be aware that internet websites listed in this work may have changed or disappeared between when this work was written and when it is read.

Unless otherwise specified, all scriptures contained herein, including quotations marked NIV, are taken from The Holy Bible, New International Version® NIV® Copyright © 1973, 1978, 1984, 2011 by Biblica, Inc. Used with permission. All rights reserved worldwide. Scripture quotations marked KJV are taken from the King James Version. Scripture quotations marked ESV are from the ESV® Bible (The Holy Bible, English Standard Version®), © 2001 by Crossway, a publishing ministry of Good News Publishers. ESV Text Edition: 2025. The ESV text may not be quoted in any publication made available to the public by a Creative Commons license. The ESV may not be translated in whole or in part into any other language. Used by permission. All rights reserved.

ISBN 978-0-9981940-4-2 Paperback
ISBN 978-0-9981940-2-8 eBook
Library of Congress Control Number: 2025943524
Published by:
ONE WAY → JESUS Publishing
805 Lake Street #374
Oak Park, Illinois 60301
www.OneWayJesusPublishing.com

*This book is dedicated to my Lord and Savior Jesus Christ
who saved my life; accepts me for the person that I am;
lifted me from poverty and caused me to stand before kings.*

I love you dearly.

Acknowledgements

I want to extend a heartfelt thank you to the following individuals...

To my father in the Lord, the late Bishop – Dr. Arthur M. Brazier, who taught me to live for Christ and gave me a strong foundation in the Apostles' Doctrine.

To my Pastor, Dr. William (Bill) Winston, who taught me the Word of Faith and helped me to learn my identity in Christ.

To my sister Rauquaia Hale-Wallace, whose encouragement, prayers, counsel, fellowship, prophetic utterances, and words of knowledge, helped me accelerate in the things of God.

To my brother in Christ, Alvin Pickett, whose fellowship, friendship, and prayers helped me go through the Refiner's fire without feeling alone.

Praise God from Whom all Blessings flow!

Table of Contents

Acknowledgements v

Introduction
Wisdom That Builds A Life 1

KEY ONE
VISION AND IMAGINATION
(What You See)

Chapter 1.1
Vision And The Power of Sight 9

Chapter 1.2
Prophetic Imagination 17

Chapter 1.3
Imagination Sanctified 25

Chapter 1.4
Faith-Filled Focus 33

KEY TWO
KNOWLEDGE
(What You Think)

Chapter 2.1
Stewarding The Mind 43

Chapter 2.2
God's Thoughts 49

Chapter 2.3
The Knowledge That Builds 55

KEY THREE
CONFESSION
(What You Say)

Chapter 3.1
The Power of Words 63

Chapter 3.2
Confessions Create Culture.. 69

Chapter 3.3
Declaring What God Said 75

KEY FOUR
WORK AND WISDOM
(What You Do)

Chapter 4.1
The Wisdom to Work It 83

Chapter 4.2
Understanding Seasons 89

Chapter 4.3
Grace for the Grind 95

Chapter 4.4
The Blessing of Work... 101

Chapter 4.5
Wisdom for Work and Wealth 107

Chapter 4.6
Multiplying with Wisdom... 113

KEY FIVE
GRATITUDE
(What You Express with Your Heart)

Chapter 5.1
The Power of Gratitude 125

Chapter 5.2
Gratitude Unlocks the Supernatural 133

Chapter 5.3
The Overflow of a Grateful Heart 141

KEY SIX
PRUDENCE
(What You Do with Your Time)

Chapter 6.1
Redeeming the Time 151

Chapter 6.2
The Wisdom of Scheduling 157

Chapter 6.3
Time, Seasons, and Discernment 163

KEY SEVEN
FORESIGHT
(What You Do with Your Money)

Chapter 7.1
Seeing Money Through Heaven's Eyes 171

Chapter 7.2
Mastering Money Before It Masters You 177

Chapter 7.3
Funding Vision with Kingdom Foresight 187

Book Summary 195

Bonus Journal
7 Stewardship Keys That Lead to Overflow 197

Activation Page
My Stewardship Commitment 200

Epilogue
A Golden Opportunity 201

About the Author 202

Introduction

Wisdom That Builds A Life

Scripture Focus:
Proverbs 4:7–8 (KJV)

"Wisdom is the principal thing; therefore get wisdom: and with all thy getting get understanding. Exalt her, and she shall promote thee: she shall bring thee to honor, when thou dost embrace her." — Proverbs 4:7–8

This book is not just about principles; it's about transformation. It's not simply a guide to better habits. It's an invitation to step into a new way of living—one rooted in **Kingdom Stewardship**, powered by **Kingdom Wisdom**, and marked by **Kingdom Overflow**.

You were never created just to survive. You were made to steward.

You were designed, anointed, and called to carry vision, lead with diligence, speak with authority, and live a life that reflects God's abundance, not just in your finances, but in your focus, your relationships, your time, and your legacy.

But in a noisy, fast-moving, success-obsessed world, it's easy to lose sight of the assignment. We get distracted by busyness. We measure success by what we accumulate rather than what we cultivate. And in the process, we often drift from what matters most: **our calling to faithfully manage what God has entrusted to us.**

This book is a recalibration. It's a return to what's eternal. It's a deep dive into what I call the **seven keys of stewardship**—seven dimensions of life that, when surrendered to God and led with wisdom, produce fruit that lasts.

Why This Book Matters Now

There's a crisis of stewardship in the body of Christ today. We have more access than ever before to tools, technology, and teaching, but still, many of us remain: Visionless. Burned out. Financially reactive. Spiritually distracted. Busy but ineffective. Gifted yet unfruitful.

It's not a lack of talent. It's not even a lack of desire. It's a lack of wisdom in how we **steward** the gifts, time, opportunities, resources, and influence we already have.

We're not waiting on more from God; **He's waiting on more from us.**

What if the breakthrough you've been praying for isn't delayed by the devil, but by disobedience in your discipline?

What if the overflow you're seeking is on the other side of reordering your life, your thoughts, your confession, your calendar, and your budget?

What if you already have enough, or even more than enough, if you'd learn to steward it well?

That's what this book is here to address.

What Is Stewardship?

In simple terms, stewardship is **managing what doesn't belong to you.** It's understanding that: Your life is not your own. Your money is not your source. Your business is not your identity. Your calling is not casual, and your time is not disposable.

You are not just an owner. **You are a steward—a manager of divine resources.**

God is the Master. We are the stewards. And from Genesis to Revelation, Scripture is clear: those who are faithful stewards are promoted, trusted, and rewarded. Not just in eternity, but here and now.

> *"Who then is the faithful and wise servant, whom the master has put in charge...?"* — Matthew 24:45

This book is not about perfection. It's about **faithfulness.** It's about learning how to multiply what God has placed in your hands and becoming the kind of person He can trust with more.

The Seven Stewardship Keys

Over the years, through Scripture study, mentorship, trial, error, and testimony, I've come to identify **seven specific areas** where stewardship makes or breaks a believer's fruitfulness.

Each chapter of this book dives into one of these seven keys:

1. **What You See — Vision and Imagination**
   Your ability to envision your future impacts how you prepare, act, and build today.

2. **What You Think — Knowledge**
   Your thoughts shape your decisions. What you feed your mind governs your direction.

3. **What You Say — Confession**
   Life and death are in the power of the tongue. Your words align your life with fear or with faith.

4. **What You Do — Work & Wisdom**
   Diligence, discipline, and discernment are the pathways to increase.

5. **What You Express — Gratitude**
   Thankfulness multiplies. Honor unlocks. Complaining costs.

6. **What You Do with Your Time — Prudence**
   You can't manufacture time, but you can waste it, spend it, or invest it.

7. **What You Do with Your Money — Foresight**
   Money reveals your trust, values, and future readiness. It's not about how much you have; it's how you steward what you already hold.

Each of these areas affects the others. Neglect one, and the rest eventually feel the impact. But if you grow in all seven, you'll become the kind of steward that can not only carry increase but sustain it with integrity.

Who This Book Is For

This book is for the entrepreneur who's tired of chasing success and wants to build a legacy; the ministry leader looking for clarity in the chaos; the creative with ideas but no structure; the parent raising Kingdom-minded children; the college student searching for direction; the burned-out believer desperate for alignment; and the visionary who sees more but doesn't know how to start.

Whether you're leading a team or leading your family... whether you're starting over or scaling up... these keys are for you.

You don't have to have it all figured out. You just have to be faithful with where you are.

The Promise of Overflow

This is not a prosperity gospel book. But it is a promise-of-the-Kingdom book. For in the Kingdom, stewardship always leads to **increase.**

"To the one who has, more will be given..." — Matthew 13:12

Faithfulness is the seedbed for multiplication. When you steward what you see, think, say, and do, **God adds His increase.** When you steward what you express, prioritize, and give, **God adds His increase.**

His increase may show up as influence, insight, income, or impact, but it will always lead to **overflow.**

This overflow is not to impress others or validate your worth, but **to fulfill your assignment.**

God doesn't just want you to be faithful; He wants you to be **fruitful.** Because fruitfulness is not just about personal gain as much as it is about feeding others, building communities, breaking cycles, and changing atmospheres.

How to Read This Book

You can read straight through. Or you can take it one chapter per week, meditate on the Scripture, journal your reflections on the questions, and pray the declarations.

Each chapter includes: a Scripture foundation, a storytelling teachingstyle section, biblical and practical examples, reflection questions, and a prayer declaration.

The goal isn't to overwhelm you; it's to **equip** you. To give you tools, not just inspiration.

Let the Holy Spirit highlight where to begin. Some of you may need to start with your money. Others with your mindset. Others still, with how you manage your time. There's no wrong place to begin, as long as you start.

Final Word Before We Begin

If you're reading this, I want to tell you something clearly: **You are already equipped. You have already been seen. You have already been chosen.**

You don't need another confirmation. You don't need to wait for a voice from the clouds. Just steward what's already in your hand. Believe what God has already said. Move with what you've already seen.

God isn't waiting for you to be perfect. He's waiting for you to be **faithful**.

So, let's go. Let's lean in. Let's learn to lead with wisdom. Let's become the kind of stewards Heaven can trust.

Let's step into a life of **stewardship that leads to overflow**.

KEY ONE

VISION AND IMAGINATION

(What You See)

Chapter 1.1

Vision And The Power of Sight

Scripture Focus:
Proverbs 29:18, Genesis 13:14–17,
Habakkuk 2:2–3

Proverbs 29:18 (KJV) *18 Where there is no vision, the people perish: but he that keepeth the law, happy is he.*

Genesis 13:14-17 (KJV) *14 And the LORD said unto Abram, after that Lot was separated from him, Lift up now thine eyes, and look from the place where thou art northward, and southward, and eastward, and westward: 15 For all the land which thou seest, to thee will I give it, and to thy seed for ever. 16 And I will make thy seed as the dust of the earth: so that if a man can number the dust of the earth, then shall thy seed also be numbered. 17 Arise, walk through the land in the length of it and in the breadth of it; for I will give it unto thee.*

Habakkuk 2:2-3 (KJV) *2 And the LORD answered me, and said, Write the vision, and make it plain upon tables, that he may run that readeth it. 3 For the vision is yet for an appointed time, but at the end it shall speak, and not lie: though it tarry, wait for it; because it will surely come, it will not tarry.*

INTRODUCTION. The Power of What You See

One of the most vital spiritual laws in the Kingdom is this: **you can't steward what you can't see.** Vision is the seed of stewardship. Every act of obedience, every resource we manage, every decision we make—it all flows from what we perceive in the Spirit.

> *"Where there is no vision, the people perish..."* — Proverbs 29:18

This verse isn't just about leadership. It's about life. When people lose sight of where they're going, they stop moving with intention. They start reacting instead of building. They settle instead of advancing. They become discouraged because they cannot see hope in their future.

But when vision is alive, people thrive. Purpose returns. Direction becomes clear. Energy follows clarity. Most importantly, stewardship begins to take shape, not just as a duty but as a divine strategy.

In this chapter, we'll explore the power of vision, how God imparts it, how the enemy attacks it, and how you can faithfully steward what God has revealed. Whether you're a pastor, business owner, parent, or artist, one thing is sure: **what you see in the Spirit will shape what you steward in your life.**

SECTION 1. Abraham—Lift Up Your Eyes

God's first major conversation with Abram after the separation from Lot wasn't about logistics. It wasn't a leadership seminar. It was an invitation to look.

> *"Lift up your eyes from where you are and look north and south, east and west. All the land that you see I will give to you..."* — Genesis 13:14–15 (NIV)

This is profound. Before God gave Abram possession, He permitted him to see.

In the Kingdom, revelation precedes acquisition.

Abraham stood on the promised ground but couldn't inherit what he refused to envision. That principle hasn't changed. God has placed gifts, relationships, ministries, and opportunities before His people, but they remain untouched because we haven't stopped to "lift our eyes."

In a world of distraction, vision becomes the rarest resource. Everything competes for your focus and attention. But vision isn't something you stumble into. You cultivate it. You steward it. You fight for it.

For the entrepreneur, this means seeing your business not just as a vehicle for income but as a kingdom tool for impact. For the pastor, it's not about building crowds; it's about building people (I would also add that the church's focus shouldn't be just on growing seating capacity but also on increasing sending capacity). For the everyday believer, it's about seeing your home, finances, and gifts through Heaven's lens.

Abraham's journey didn't begin with a roadmap. It started with a revelation. The same will be true for you.

SECTION 2. Habakkuk—Write the Vision

"Then the Lord answered me and said: Write the vision and make it plain on tablets, that he may run who reads it." — Habakkuk 2:2 (NKJV)

God didn't just tell Habakkuk to receive the vision; He instructed him to write it. Why? Because what stays in your head dies in your head; what you fail to write, you will eventually forget. But what is written becomes transferable, trackable, and able to be stewarded.

Writing the vision serves several critical purposes:
- **Clarity:** The act of writing forces you to think. You must translate inspiration into language. Fuzzy vision becomes clear on paper.
- **Focus:** When everything feels urgent, a written vision reminds you of what's essential.
- **Accountability:** Written goals can be measured and reviewed. They hold you to your confession.
- **Transferability:** Others can't run with a vision they can't read. If you want to build a team, launch a ministry, or grow a business, you must make the vision plain.

God doesn't give us a vision to admire. He gives it to us to run with.

You don't need a 50-page business plan to obey God, but you do need clarity. That may be a journal. A vision board. A whiteboard in your office. But somewhere, it must live in writing.

Vision written becomes vision weaponized.

So, what's written in your house right now? What are your children reading? What are you training your employees on? What are you reviewing when you get discouraged?

A steward doesn't just receive vision. A steward writes it.

SECTION 3. Nehemiah—Vision Will Be Attacked

When Nehemiah returned to rebuild the walls of Jerusalem, they greeted him with mockery, not applause.

Sanballat and Tobiah laughed, and the rest doubted the possibility. Rumors, sabotage, and fatigue set in. But Nehemiah refused to come down from the wall. In the same way, we must refuse to come down from what we see.

"I am doing a great work, and I cannot come down." — Nehemiah 6:3

Every great vision will face warfare. And often, that warfare won't come from strangers; it'll come from within.

Internal doubt. External pressure. Family disapproval. Financial limitations. Burnout and the temptation to compromise.

The enemy of your vision is not always the devil. Sometimes, it's distraction.

Stewarding vision means guarding your focus. It means knowing what wall you're building and refusing to come down.

Nehemiah finished the wall in just 52 days, not because he had the best tools but because he had unshakable focus.

Faithful stewards protect their focus like warriors guard their gates.

SECTION 4. Joseph—Vision Requires Process

Joseph's story is one of the most vivid portraits of vision in all of scripture. As a teenager, he received a dream from God. In the dream, his family bowed before him. It was a vision of leadership and influence.

However, the next 13 years didn't resemble leadership at all.

His brothers betrayed him. Sold into slavery. Falsely accused and thrown into prison. Forgotten by the very people he helped.

And yet, **God was still working on the vision.**

What God shows you doesn't always match what you're walking through. And that's where stewardship becomes hard. Because when what you see spiritually and what you experience naturally are in conflict, you'll be tempted to give up.

But Joseph never let go of the vision. In time, the vision came to pass exactly as God said.

"You meant it for evil, but God meant it for good..." — Genesis 50:20

Vision is tested in the hallway between the promise and the palace. That hallway is where most people let go.

But faithful stewards stay in the process. They interpret other people's dreams in prison, knowing theirs will manifest in time. They serve with excellence in even the most minor roles. They resist bitterness. They remain available.

You don't graduate to greatness because you saw it. You get there because you **stewarded what God showed you, even when it didn't feel like it was working.**

SECTION 5. Paul—Obedient to the Heavenly Vision

When Paul stood before King Agrippa in Acts 26, he summarized his life in a single sentence:

"I was not disobedient to the heavenly vision." — Acts 26:19

That's a stunning statement because Paul had endured shipwrecks, floggings, stoning, hunger, prison, and betrayal. Yet he measured success not by comfort but by obedience.

Vision isn't about how much money you make, how many people you reach, or how big your platform grows. Vision is about **alignment**. Are you doing what God showed you? Are you living the life He revealed to you?

For businesspeople, this means you don't chase every trend. You stay rooted in the purpose God gave you. For church leaders, it means you don't imitate someone else's church; you build the one He told you to create. For creatives, it means you write, design, or develop what God breathed into you, not what gets clicks.

God measures the stewardship of your vision by obedience, not optics.

SECTION 6. Jesus—For the Joy Set Before Him

Even Jesus was fueled by vision.

> *"For the joy that was set before Him, He endured the cross..."* — Hebrews 12:2

That's staggering. Jesus endured betrayal, bloodshed, humiliation, and crucifixion because He had **a clear picture** of what was to come. The joy that was set before Him was the vision of you and me redeemed, restored, and reconciled to the Father.

Heaven's King was stewarding a vision of salvation.

And that vision gave Him endurance.

If Jesus needed vision to finish His assignment, we certainly must not think that we can finish ours without it.

The cross didn't look like victory, but vision let Him see the resurrection on the other side. Your current challenge may not feel like purpose, but vision will keep you walking toward what's ahead.

A faith-filled vision gives strength to steward your calling through any storm.

SECTION 7. Practical Tools for Stewarding Vision

Stewardship isn't just about revelation; it's about responsibility.

Here are some **practical tools** to help you steward what God shows you:

1. **Vision Journal**
   Dedicate a notebook to the things God shows you. Write down scriptures, dreams, prophetic words, and divine ideas. Review it monthly.
2. **The "Next Step" List**
   Every vision should be accompanied by your next 1–3 action steps. Not everything will happen at once. But vision without movement stagnates.

3. **Wise Counsel Check-ins**
   Meet monthly or quarterly with a mentor, pastor, or trusted advisor. Share your vision. Let them challenge your blind spots and confirm direction.
4. **Vision Review Retreat**
   Once a year, take a few days away to pray, fast, and revisit your vision. What's still relevant? What needs updating? What's ready for bold action?
5. **Declare It Daily**
   Speak what God has shown you aloud. Let your confession align with His promise, even when circumstances don't.

You can only sustain your Vision through repetition, review, and realignment.

SECTION 8. Reflection Questions

Take time to sit with these before God and in your journal:

1. What vision has God given me that I've neglected or forgotten?
2. Where have I allowed distractions to blur my focus?
3. Have I written the vision clearly enough for others to run with?
4. Am I more focused on results than on faithfulness?
5. What's the next simple step I can take to honor what God has shown me?

SECTION 9. Closing Reflection & Activation

The vision of a steward is to see like Abraham—before the land is yours, before the crowd believes, and before it looks possible. What you see could enable you to **multiply what is before you, not just manage it.**

SECTION 10. Prayer Declaration

Father, thank You for divine vision. I repent for the times I ignored or doubted what You revealed. Open the eyes of my heart. Restore my spiritual sight. Give me the courage to write, protect, and act on what You've shown me. I declare clarity, consistency, and obedience. I will not come down from the wall. I will run with the vision. In Jesus' name, amen.

Chapter 1.2

Prophetic Imagination

Scripture Focus:
Joel 2:28, Exodus 31:1–5, Romans 4:17

Joel 2:28 (KJV) *28 And it shall come to pass afterward, that I will pour out my spirit upon all flesh; and your sons and your daughters shall prophesy, your old men shall dream dreams, your young men shall see visions:*

Exodus 31:1-5 (KJV) *1 And the LORD spake unto Moses, saying, 2 See, I have called by name Bezaleel the son of Uri, the son of Hur, of the tribe of Judah: 3 And I have filled him with the spirit of God, in wisdom, and in understanding, and in knowledge, and in all manner of workmanship, 4 To devise cunning works, to work in gold, and in silver, and in brass, 5 And in cutting of stones, to set them, and in carving of timber, to work in all manner of workmanship.*

Romans 4:17 (KJV) *17 (As it is written, I have made thee a father of many nations,) before him whom he believed, even God, who quickeneth the dead, and calleth those things which be not as though they were.*

INTRODUCTION. How God Uses Creative Minds

In a world driven by data, logic, and production, many underestimate the power of imagination. Yet the first chapter of the Bible begins with creativity—God seeing what didn't exist and speaking it into being. That same Spirit that hovered over the void now dwells in us, empowering us not only to manage what exists but to envision what could be. This envisioning, powered by the Spirit, is the essence of prophetic imagination. It's not just creativity for creativity's sake—it's seeing with God's eyes and building what He reveals.

When God chose someone to design the Tabernacle, He didn't pick a warrior or a theologian—He chose an artist named Bezalel. Why? Because God values when we submit our imagination to His Spirit. Bezalel was "filled with the Spirit of God, with wisdom, understanding, knowledge, and all kinds of skills" (Exodus 31:1–5). He became a model of what it looks like to create under divine direction, where inspiration and instruction meet. This story reminds us that in the Kingdom, creativity is not just permitted; it's anointed.

Prophetic imagination is a divine gift, a Spirit-empowered ability to see beyond what is and into what God says can be. Noah imagined a boat when rain was a myth. David dreamed of a temple he wouldn't live to build. John saw eternity and nations in Revelation. Paul wrote letters envisioning churches that did not yet exist. These were not hallucinations. They were blueprints for divine activity on Earth, given to people with hearts willing to see, write, and act.

In this chapter, we'll unpack what prophetic imagination truly is—not fantasy or escapism, but a fusion of faith and foresight. It's a tool of stewardship that helps us co-create with God. The same Spirit that hovered over the waters in Genesis now hovers over your ideas, prompting you to shape the unseen. Romans 4:17 says God "calls those things that do not exist as though they did." He invites us to do the same.

But imagination isn't enough. We must combine it with wisdom. Bezalel received not only inspiration but also understanding, knowledge, and skill.

Daniel exemplified this as well; he possessed both prophetic insight and practical strategies for kings. In today's world, especially for Kingdom entrepreneurs and leaders, this balance is crucial. It's not just about dreaming—it's about designing and delivering with excellence.

Of course, every creative steward must guard their imagination. Our creativity can become self-serving if it ever becomes separated from God. That's why intimacy with God is vital. We must ask: Did this idea come from prayer or pressure? Does it align with Scripture? Will it serve others or only elevate me? Integrity, intimacy, and impact are the three safeguards that ensure our imagination stays on assignment.

In the end, you are more than a receiver of divine ideas—you're a carrier. A builder. A co-creator. Prophetic imagination is not only reserved for pastors or prophets; it's for artists, business owners, parents, musicians, and strategists. It's for you.

This chapter will stir you to dream again, to build boldly, and to steward the Kingdom's blueprints with practical wisdom and prophetic courage.

SECTION 1. Bezalel: The Kingdom's Blueprint in a Craftsman's Hands

When God revealed the design for the Tabernacle—the sacred dwelling place that would host His glory—He gave it not to a priest or a prophet but to an artist. Bezalel, the son of Uri, was filled with the Spirit of God, endowed with wisdom, understanding, and skill to bring a divine vision into physical reality (Exodus 31:1–5).

This detail is not incidental. It reveals that the Spirit's outpouring isn't reserved for preachers and prophets but for artisans, designers, craftspeople, and builders. Bezalel didn't simply decorate—he interpreted the unseen. He stewarded a revelation and translated it into textures, tones, fabrics, and functions. In Bezalel, we see the heart of prophetic imagination at work.

God doesn't merely want worship from the Tabernacle; He wants stewardship in its construction. He chooses people with **spiritual eyes and skilled hands** to shape spaces where Heaven can dwell.

SECTION 2. Prophetic Imagination Defined

Prophetic imagination is the Spirit-inspired capacity to envision God's future and co-labor in shaping it. It is not fantasy—it's **faith-based foresight**. It looks at what currently exists and boldly declares, *"There is more."*

It's the blueprint before the building. The melody before the music. The sketch before the sculpture. The divine spark before anything takes form.

As Joel prophesied, *"Your sons and daughters will prophesy, your old men will dream dreams, your young men will see visions"* (Joel 2:28). The implication is not just spiritual expression but creative co-participation with the Kingdom's unfolding agenda.

Prophetic imagination calls things that are not as though they were (Romans 4:17). It's what enables Kingdom-minded people to start ministries, launch businesses, compose music, write books, design software, and birth movements—not out of mere ambition, but out of obedience to a heavenly picture.

SECTION 3. Faith Is the Framework

All true creativity in the Kingdom begins with a picture in the spirit. Faith gives substance to that picture (Hebrews 11:1). Without faith, imagination becomes escapism. But with faith, imagination becomes **stewardship.**

Consider Noah: he had never seen rain yet built a boat for a flood no one could imagine. Consider David: he dreamed of building a house for the Lord even though he wasn't the one to construct it. Consider Paul: he wrote letters to churches that didn't yet exist, with leaders he may never meet again on this side of Heaven.

In each case, they saw something beyond their current reality and **acted accordingly.**

Prophetic imagination must be rooted in the Word, refined by the Spirit, and expressed through obedience. It is not wishful thinking. It is **vision in motion.**

SECTION 4. Imagination as a Stewardship Tool

In Kingdom leadership, imagination is not childish; it's essential. You can't build what you haven't seen. You can't steward what you haven't envisioned. The architect's first tool is not a hammer; it's a blueprint. Likewise, the steward's first step isn't execution; it's insight.

Lack of imagination and insight is where many believers fall short. They wait for clarity but never cultivate imagination. They look for opportunity but haven't dared to picture what's possible. They want divine outcomes without a creative process.

But God has always worked through those who will see, design, and build.

To steward imagination well means:
- Making time to dream in God's presence
- Writing down what He shows you
- Building prototypes of purpose—even if they're messy at first

- Allowing your communion with God, not competition, to fuel your creative process

Your imagination is not a playground for ego; it's a workshop for worship.

SECTION 5. **The Role of Discipline and Skill**

Bezalel wasn't just inspired—he was skilled.

The Holy Spirit filled him, yes, but God also trained his hands. He knew how to work with gold, silver, stone, and wood. Prophetic imagination without **craftsmanship** is just inspiration. But you produce excellence when you combine vision with discipline.

Lack of consistency is where many visionary believers stop short. They have the dream but lack the diligence. But faithful stewards don't just see—they **sharpen.** They develop their skill, commit to their training, seek counsel, and pursue growth with humility.

As Paul wrote to Timothy, *"Fan into flame the gift of God within you..."* (2 Timothy 1:6). That's stewardship—turning a spark into a flame, a dream into development.

The Church must reclaim the value of craftsmanship, where our practice, not just our passion, refines our imagination.

SECTION 6. **Guarding the Wellspring**

Imagination is powerful. But like any gift, we must guard it.

A steward must be mindful of what feeds the imagination. We live in a content-heavy world where screens dominate, and culture screams for attention. If we aren't careful, our creative lens can become fogged by:
- Social comparison
- Carnal inspiration
- Fear-based content
- Cultural pressure

A steward of imagination is selective about input. They filter media. They protect silence. They value solitude. They understand that the clearest creativity flows from **communion.**

Jesus often withdrew to lonely places. Not because He lacked content but because He valued clarity.

Likewise, we fuel our prophetic imagination by nearness, not noise.

SECTION 7. Imagination That Builds the Kingdom

Prophetic imagination isn't just about personal impact—it's about **Kingdom advancement.**

When God gives you a picture of something that doesn't exist yet, it's not for your ego; it's for others' benefit. What you build may house His presence. What you write may deliver healing. What you compose may lead worshippers to a breakthrough.

Creative stewards understand that their output is not about fame but **fruit.**

- That curriculum you're designing? It may disciple thousands.
- That tech idea? It may fund missions.
- That art series? It may restore dignity and hope to broken hearts.
- That family rhythm you create? It may bring generational change.

The world doesn't just need more content. It needs **consecrated imagination.**

God made you to build courageously by seeing things differently. He wants to release Heaven into the Earth through you.

SECTION 8. Reflection Questions

1. What has God shown me in the secret place that I've not yet written down or pursued?
2. Have I treated my imagination as holy ground, or have I neglected it?
3. What disciplines can I adopt to strengthen my creative capacity?
4. Is my vision aligned with the Kingdom or driven by ambition?
5. Who needs what God has shown me to create?

SECTION 9. Declaration Prayer

Lord, thank You for the gift of imagination. I consecrate my mind to You. I receive the vision You've placed in me. I reject comparison, fear, and confusion. Anoint my creativity. Let my ideas align with Your Kingdom. Make me a builder of things unseen and a steward of the blueprints You release. In Jesus' name, amen.

Chapter 1.3

Imagination Sanctified

Scripture Focus:
Genesis 11:6, Romans 12:2, Ephesians 3:20

Genesis 11:6 (KJV) *6 And the LORD said, Behold, the people is one, and they have all one language; and this they begin to do: and now nothing will be restrained from them, which they have imagined to do.*

Romans 12:2 (KJV) *2 And be not conformed to this world: but be ye transformed by the renewing of your mind, that ye may prove what is that good, and acceptable, and perfect, will of God.*

Ephesians 3:20 (KJV) *20 Now unto him that is able to do exceeding abundantly above all that we ask or think, according to the power that worketh in us,*

INTRODUCTION. The Gift of a Creative Mind

Imagination is one of the most overlooked forms of stewardship. Most of the world considers imagination to be something childish or whimsical. But in the Kingdom of God, **imagination is a tool for dominion.** The Bible says in Ephesians 3:20:
"Now unto him who is able to do exceedingly abundantly above all that we ask or think, according to the power that worketh in us..."

The word "think" in Greek is *noieō* — to perceive, ponder, imagine. This Scripture means God works beyond your imagination, but not apart from it. **If you can't imagine it, you likely won't pursue it.**

The enemy knows this. That's why one of his most effective strategies is to corrupt your imagination. He'll fill it with fear, worst-case scenarios, guilt, fantasy, lust, and pride—anything to hijack your creative power.

But when your imagination is sanctified, it becomes a prophetic canvas. You begin to **see what God sees**, not just with your eyes, but with your spirit. And that, my friend, is where supernatural stewardship begins.

SECTION 1. The Tower of Babel— Imagination with Unity

In Genesis 11:6, we find a profound truth tucked inside a judgment story:

"And the Lord said, Behold, the people is one, and they have all one language; and this they begin to do: and now nothing will be restrained from them, which they have imagined to do."

God Himself acknowledged the **power of unified imagination**. These were not godly people. Their intentions were rebellious. Yet, even in disobedience, their **mental agreement created momentum**.

"Nothing will be restrained from them, which they have imagined to do."

Imagine that. God didn't say, "Nothing they build." He said, "Nothing they **imagine**." That means they have to build it twice—they must build it in their imagination before building it with their hands. If they do it that way, then "Nothing will be restrained from them, which they have imagined to do."

It also means imagination is a force that either builds Babel or builds the Kingdom. It's not neutral—it's directional.

In business, imagination becomes strategy. In ministry, imagination becomes innovation. In a family, imagination becomes a legacy. In prayer, imagination becomes a vision.

When people imagine together, they build faster. When sanctified leaders bring teams into shared imagination, it becomes a **prophetic culture**.

But what happens when imagination is unsanctified? It spirals into control, fear, or fantasy. People imagine failure, betrayal, catastrophe. They imagine worst-case scenarios and call it "being realistic." But the problem isn't imagination; it's that their imagination hasn't been made holy.

So, the question isn't whether *you have imagination*. The question is: **Who owns your imagination? Who is the source inspiring it? Who is it yielded to?**

SECTION 2. Transformation Begins in the Mind

"Do not be conformed to this world, but be transformed by the renewing of your mind..." — Romans 12:2

The battlefield of transformation is the mind. That includes your imagination. It's not just about behavior change. It's about **mental renovation**.

To renew means to:
- Strip out the old
- Rebuild structure
- Replace faulty ideas with truth

Most believers don't have a discipline problem. They have a **thinking problem**. And underneath that is often an **imagination problem**.

When your imagination is unrenewed:
- You shrink back from opportunities
- You assume failure before you start
- You envision rejection, not favor
- You imagine cycles, not breakthrough

But when you **yield your imagination to the Holy Spirit**, it becomes a sanctified source of creative instruction.

A sanctified imagination imagines:
- Kingdom Expansion
- Reconciliation
- Generational Blessing
- Innovative business ideas
- Souls saved
- Solutions to impossible problems

Sanctified imagination is how Paul could write prison letters full of joy and vision. He saw beyond the bars. His imagination was alive even when his body was chained.

The renewing of your imagination may be the most crucial breakthrough you never realized you needed.

SECTION 3. Imagination in the Life of David

David was not just a warrior; he was a worshiper, poet, and visionary king. Before he ever ruled, he imagined. Sitting in shepherd fields, he envisioned deliverance, greatness, and glory for God.

> *"The Lord is my Shepherd; I shall not want..."* — Psalm 23:1

That wasn't just doctrine—it was divine imagination. David pictured God walking with him through green pastures, through valleys, through battlefields, and into victory. His mind wasn't stuck on the sheep in front of him. He anchored his soul to the **presence of God within him.**

When David approached Goliath, he had a picture of victory. The army of Israel saw themselves as grasshoppers. David saw himself as God's champion. The difference wasn't armor. The difference was imagination sanctified by faith.

Your mindset determines your strategy. David didn't come with a sword; he came with a sling. He didn't fight like Saul; he fought like David because he had a different image in his heart.

You will never steward God's vision for your life if you fill your imagination with defeat. **You must see yourself as God sees you before anyone else does.**

SECTION 4. How the Enemy Pollutes the Mind

The enemy cannot create, but he can **corrupt**. His weapon of choice is suggestion. He feeds fear through false images. He leads believers into worry through worst-case projections.

False images are the reason why Paul writes:

> *"Casting down imaginations, and every high thing that exalteth itself against the knowledge of God..."* — 2 Corinthians 10:5

The word "imaginations" in Greek is *logismos* — reasoning, thought patterns, mental constructs. The enemy doesn't always tempt you with evil; he traps you with limitation.

Here's what a polluted imagination looks like:
- You picture your business failing before it launches
- You imagine people rejecting your leadership

- You replay past trauma as your permanent future
- You envision constant struggle as your "portion."

But here's the truth: **the devil doesn't get to define your imagination unless you give him the pen.**

The moment you surrender your thought life to Christ, the rewriting begins. You start seeing purpose in pain. You start picturing reconciliation in broken relationships. You start dreaming again—not just for yourself, but for others.

That's how sanctified imagination becomes warfare.

SECTION 5. Creative Thinking as Prophetic Expression

Many people assume prophecy is only verbal — "Thus says the Lord." But often, prophecy is expressed **through creative thought.**

When God gives a person a divine idea — a painting, a business concept, a new model of ministry, a book title, a product blueprint — it is **prophetic imagination** at work. It's seeing something that doesn't exist in the natural realm and stewarding it until it becomes reality.

Most of what God intends for the earth is not visible and has not yet arrived. It will take prophetic imagination and stewardship to bring them to fruition.

"Call to me and I will answer you and tell you great and unsearchable things you do not know." — Jeremiah 33:3

God doesn't just answer with facts; He answers with truth. **He answers with light.** He answers with revelation — divine imagination revealed.

A sanctified imagination makes space for:
- Inspired solutions in the boardroom
- God-breathed ideas for your marketing strategy
- Worship songs that release healing
- Curriculum that shifts a generation
- Financial strategies that break poverty cycles

Your imagination isn't carnal when it's submitted and yielded to God; it's **prophetic.**

We need more believers who stop asking, "What's allowed?" and start asking, "God, what do You want to create through me?"

SECTION 6. **Practical Tools to Sanctify Your Mind**

Sanctifying your imagination is not automatic. It requires intentional stewardship. Here are five tools to help you daily:

1. **Mindset Check**
   Each morning, ask: "What's dominating my imagination right now?" Is it fear? Faith? Hope? Regret?

2. **Word Immersion**
   The more Scripture you read, the more God reshapes your mental framework. The Word uproots lies and plants truth.

3. **Image Discipline**
   Be mindful of what you consume visually. Social media, entertainment, ads—they all feed the imagination. Starve what pollutes. Feed what fuels.

4. **Holy Spirit Dialogue**
   Ask the Holy Spirit to give you Heaven's perspective. Imagination aligned with His presence produces power.

5. **Creative Practice**
   Set aside time each week to dream with God. Journal, sketch, brainstorm, and pray in the Spirit with a pen in your hand. Let Him paint on the canvas of your heart.

SECTION 7. **Reflection Questions**

Take time to consider and write your responses:

1. What do I most often imagine — fear or faith?
2. When was the last time I gave God space to shape my imagination?
3. What images, thoughts, or memories do I need to surrender to Him today?
4. What creative expression might God want to birth through me?

SECTION 8. Prayer Declaration

Father, I thank You for the gift of imagination. I surrender my thoughts, dreams, and inner images to You. Purify my imagination. Remove the residue of fear, trauma, and limitation. I receive the mind of Christ. I ask You to speak, to show, and to lead me into visions that align with Your will. Let my thoughts create life. Let my creativity bring glory to You. In Jesus' name, amen.

Chapter 1.4

Faith-Filled Focus

Scripture Focus
Hebrews 12:1–2, Philippians 3:13–14, Matthew 14:28–31

Hebrews 12:1-2 (KJV) *1.Wherefore seeing we also are compassed about with so great a cloud of witnesses, let us lay aside every weight, and the sin which doth so easily beset us, and let us run with patience the race that is set before us, 2. Looking unto Jesus the author and finisher of our faith; who for the joy that was set before him endured the cross, despising the shame, and is set down at the right hand of the throne of God.*

Philippians 3:13-14 (KJV) *13. Brethren, I count not myself to have apprehended: but this one thing I do, forgetting those things which are behind, and reaching forth unto those things which are before, 14. I press toward the mark for the prize of the high calling of God in Christ Jesus.*

Matthew 14:28-31 (KJV) *28. And Peter answered him and said, Lord, if it be thou, bid me come unto thee on the water. 29. And he said, Come. And when Peter was come down out of the ship, he walked on the water, to go to Jesus. 30. But when he saw the wind boisterous, he was afraid; and beginning to sink, he cried, saying, Lord, save me. 31. And immediately Jesus stretched forth his hand, and caught him, and said unto him, O thou of little faith, wherefore didst thou doubt?*

INTRODUCTION. **The Fight to Stay Focused**

If vision is what you see, then focus is what you **stay fixed on**.

In today's culture, focus is rare. 'Stealing your attention' is engineered into everything. Notifications from social media, obligations at work, entertainment on various platforms, pressure from societal expectations—it's all noise. But in the Kingdom, **faith-filled focus is not optional.** It's essential for fruitfulness.

God may have given you a divine vision, but **it's your unwavering focus that ultimately determines your finish.**

Hebrews 12:2 tells us to fix our eyes on Jesus—the author and finisher of our faith. Why? Because the one you focus on is the one you follow. **Focus fuels movement. Distraction delays destiny.**

Focus isn't about personality type; it's about spiritual maturity. It's about saying:

"God, I choose to lock in. I refuse to be moved by fear, fatigue, or feelings. I will run the race with my eyes on You."

In this chapter, we'll uncover how to protect your focus, guard your energy, and persevere with clarity so that your vision produces results.

SECTION 1. **Eyes on Jesus—The Example of Faith**

> "...Let us run with endurance the race that is set before us, looking unto Jesus, the author and finisher of our faith..." — Hebrews 12:1–2

This verse teaches something profound: **you can't run well if you're not looking well.**

Focus is directional. You can't walk one way while staring in another way. When we fix our eyes on Jesus, we're not just gazing; we're anchoring.

Jesus endured betrayal, torture, and the cross because He saw "the joy set before Him." He had a picture of redemption that overpowered His pain. His focus wasn't on the nails; it was on the outcome. That's how He could endure.

For us, focus is a choice to keep our eyes on Him, **not the critics, not the chaos, not the calendar.**

You may be leading a church, managing a team, parenting teenagers, or building a business. But the question is: *what are you looking at while you do it?*
- Are your eyes on the problem or the promise?
- On your limits or God's sufficiency?
- On the storm or the Savior?

Faith-filled focus is not passive—it's intentional. It's a deliberate action that helps you keep your mind from spiraling, your emotions from crashing, and your decisions from detouring.

Jesus is not just the beginning of your faith; He's the focus that gets you through.

SECTION 2. Peter on the Water—The Cost of Distraction

In Matthew 14, Peter did something no other disciple dared to do—he walked on water.

> *"Peter got down out of the boat, walked on the water and came toward Jesus. But when he saw the wind, he was afraid and, beginning to sink..."* — Matthew 14:29–30

Peter walked on water **as long as he focused on Jesus.** The moment he looked at the wind, he began to sink.

The problem wasn't the wind. It had been there the whole time. The problem was Peter's **shift in focus.**

Distraction will always cause you to sink faster than weakness. Many leaders don't burn out because they're overworked—they burn out because they're **over-stimulated** and **under-focused.**

Peter had supernatural momentum until his focus fractured.
- How often do we start in faith but begin to sink when fear hits?
- How often do we let the storm become more real than the Savior?

Focus doesn't mean the storms stop. It means the storms stop shaping your decisions.

If you want to walk in supernatural success, you must learn to **focus through the noise.**

SECTION 3. Paul—Forgetting What's Behind

"One thing I do: Forgetting what is behind and straining toward what is ahead, I press on..." — Philippians 3:13–14

Paul understood that **focus requires forgetting**. You cannot press forward while clinging to what's behind. Yesterday's victories and yesterday's failures can both become distractions if they dominate your attention.

For Paul, forgetting didn't mean erasing memories. It meant refusing to let them define his direction. His focus was on the *upward call* — the divine assignment ahead of him.

Many believers are stuck because they are gazing backward:

- Replaying what didn't work
- Reliving who walked away
- Rehearsing what hurt them
- Regretting what they didn't do

But Paul said, "**This one thing I do...**" Focus isn't about multitasking—it's about mastery.

When you try to focus on too many things, you dilute your faith. But when you commit to one thing—one calling, one step, one Word—you build momentum. This commitment empowers you, giving you the strength to push forward.

Faithful stewardship means focusing on the future outcome and not being trapped by hindsight.

SECTION 4. The Enemies of Focus

If God uses focus to move you forward, you can be sure the enemy will use distraction to hold you back.

Here are five common enemies of faith-filled focus:

1. **Comparison**
   Looking at what others are building, leading, or achieving will cloud your clarity. You cannot run your race while watching someone else's.

2. **Busyness**
   Not all activity is obedience. The devil doesn't have to make you bad—he just has to make you busy. Focus dies where the margin is missing.

3. **Offense**
   Nothing derails vision like a wounded heart. When you nurse a grudge, you rehearse pain. And what you rehearse, you focus on.

4. **Unclear Vision**
   Without a compelling "why," your energy will scatter. Focus needs a target. Lack of clarity creates distraction by default.

5. **Fear of Missing Out**
   We chase every opportunity because we're afraid of missing "the big one." But in the Kingdom, **God honors faithfulness over frantic movement.**

A focused life is a fruitful life. You can't focus on everything. But you must focus on something, and it better be eternal.

SECTION 5. The Power of "One Thing"

Throughout Scripture, we see the phrase "one thing" used repeatedly. It's a thread of focused living woven through lives of significant impact.

> *"One thing I ask of the Lord... that I may dwell in the house of the Lord..."* — Psalm 27:4

> *"One thing you lack..."* — Mark 10:21

> *"One thing I do..."* — Philippians 3:13

> *"Only one thing is necessary..."* — Luke 10:42

God blesses singular focus. **When you know your "one thing" in a season, everything else falls into place.**

For Mary, it was sitting at Jesus' feet. For David, it was seeking God's presence. For Paul, it was pressing forward. For Jesus, it was finishing His Father's work.

So, what's *your* one thing right now?

Not your five-year plan. Not your someday goal. What's the one thing you are to focus on **today**?

Focus isn't about limitation; it's about alignment. When your focus aligns with the Kingdom, grace follows.

SECTION 6. Tools to Strengthen Your Focus

Here are practical ways to stay focused when distractions abound:

1. **The Morning Lock-In**
   Empower yourself by starting each day with the question: *"Lord, what's my assignment today?"* Then, you may want to write it down and keep it visible, setting the tone for a focused and productive day.

2. **The Vision Reminder**
   Stay inspired and motivated by placing your God-given vision in places where your eyes often go, like your mirror, phone screen, or dashboard. Focus requires visual reinforcement, and your visual reinforcement will keep you on track.

3. **The Margin Reset**
   Schedule time to do *nothing* but be still before God. Silence strengthens clarity. Distraction often thrives in noise.

4. **The Accountability Partner**
   Tell a trusted friend or mentor your focus goal for the week. Let them hold you to it. Focus flourishes with support.

5. **The Yes/No Filter**
   Before taking on any new opportunity, ask: *"Does this align with my focus in this season?"* If not, let it go.

SECTION 7. Reflection Questions

1. What is God calling me to focus on in this season?
2. What distractions have been pulling my energy and attention?
3. What voices or platforms am I looking at that are blurring my clarity?
4. How can I structure my week to reflect focus instead of frenzy?

SECTION 8. **Prayer Declaration**

Father, I thank You for the gift of focus. I fix my eyes on You—above every fear, beyond every distraction. I repent for letting worry, comparison, and busyness cloud my calling. Refine my focus. Show me my "one thing" in this season. I declare clarity, discipline, and unwavering attention to what You've assigned me. I will not sink in the storm. I will not look away. My eyes are on You. In Jesus' name, amen.

KEY TWO

KNOWLEDGE

(What You Think)

Chapter 2.1

Stewarding The Mind

Scripture Focus
Romans 12:2, Philippians 4:8, 2 Corinthians 10:5

Romans 12:2 (KJV) *2 And be not conformed to this world: but be ye transformed by the renewing of your mind, that ye may prove what is that good, and acceptable, and perfect, will of God.*

Philippians 4:8 (KJV) *8 Finally, brethren, whatsoever things are true, whatsoever things are honest, whatsoever things are just, whatsoever things are pure, whatsoever things are lovely, whatsoever things are of good report; if there be any virtue, and if there be any praise, think on these things.*

2 Corinthians 10:5 (KJV) *5 Casting down imaginations, and every high thing that exalteth itself against the knowledge of God, and bringing into captivity every thought to the obedience of Christ;*

INTRODUCTION. Why the Mind Matters

The mind is the gateway to destiny. You cannot steward your life, your resources, or your calling if you don't learn to **steward your thoughts**.

"Be transformed by the renewing of your mind..." — Romans 12:2

Everything God wants to do through you must first be processed **in you.** Before transformation shows up in your behavior, it begins in your mind.

The devil knows this. That's why his greatest war isn't in your circumstances; it's in your **thought life.** If he can shape your thinking, he can shape your decisions. If he can shape your choices, he can shape your direction. And if he shapes your direction, he hijacks your destiny.

But the good news is **you're not powerless.** God has given you authority, wisdom, and spiritual weapons to **take control of your mind**—to break old patterns, build truth-based thinking, and live from a renewed mindset.

This chapter will help you:
- Identify toxic thoughts
- Replace them with truth
- Build a mental framework that aligns with God's purpose

Because until you surrender your mind to God, He will not transform your life.

SECTION 1. Romans 12—Renewal Before Transformation

"Do not be conformed to this world, but be transformed by the renewing of your mind..." — Romans 12:2

This verse doesn't say, *"Be transformed"* by trying harder. It says, *"Be transformed" by thinking differently.*

Belief is not just a catalyst; it's the powerhouse for transformation. **It's not about changing your behavior but about changing your belief system.** By altering your perspective on God, yourself, others, success, failure, purpose, and destiny, you can truly change your life.

The Greek word for "renewing" is *anakainosis*—a complete renovation. Not a touch-up. A tear-down-and-rebuild. In this process, God is not just an observer but an active participant. He wants to gut the old way of thinking and install His Kingdom's blueprint, which is a divine plan for your life, filled with love, purpose, and fulfillment. Your role is to align your thoughts and actions with His plan.

Here's what that looks like:
- Old Thought: *"I'll never be enough."* Renewed Thought: *"I am complete in Christ."*
- Old Thought: *"This will never change."* Renewed Thought: *"With God, all things are possible."*
- Old Thought: *"I don't know what I'm doing."* Renewed Thought: *"I have the mind of Christ."*

Remember, **your mind is the control center of your destiny.** It's not just about adopting new habits; it's about installing a whole new operating system. You have the power to release or restrict your calling, your future, and your destiny.

SECTION 2. **2 Corinthians 10—Taking Thoughts Captive**

"...take every thought captive to obey Christ." — 2 Corinthians 10:5

Your mind is not a highway for any thought to ride through. It's a fortress, a place of security, and **you're the gatekeeper,** ensuring only the right thoughts enter.

Every day, thoughts come:
- Some are from God
- Some are from your flesh
- Some are from the enemy

You can't always control what shows up, but you can control what stays.

Taking thoughts captive means:
- Interrogating thoughts that don't match God's truth
- Rejecting lies and replacing them with Scripture
- Refusing to meditate on what God never said

When a thought comes in that says, *"You're not good enough,"* You don't just sit with it; you **bind it, reject it, and speak the truth back, asserting your control over your mind.**

When you take every thought captive, you're engaging in spiritual warfare—it's won in the mind. So, be always ready to fight.

SECTION 3. **The Cost of a Neglected Mind**

A neglected mind is like an unguarded city—vulnerable, chaotic, and eventually overrun.

When you don't steward your thoughts:
- Fear multiplies
- Anxiety becomes normal
- Confusion sets in

- Depression gains ground
- Bitterness festers
- Pride subtly takes root

Many believers are spiritually strong but mentally weak—not because they lack faith, but because they've abandoned their thought life.

They pray with power on Sunday but spiral into fear by Monday. They believe God's promises with their mouth but rehearse lies in their mind.

Why? Because **your mind must be discipled too.**

Just like your heart needs prayer, your mind needs renewal. Just like your spirit needs the Word of God, your mind needs **mental alignment**.

If you don't feed your mind with truth, it will feast on whatever the world offers. And when the mind is malnourished, the soul becomes unstable.

You cannot steward your assignment if your thought life is unsubmitted.

SECTION 4. Philippians 4—Think on These Things

"Whatever is true, noble, right, pure, lovely, admirable—think about such things." — Philippians 4:8

Paul doesn't just tell us what to stop thinking—he tells us what to start thinking.

Thinking higher thoughts is not just a matter of wishful thinking; it's a fundamental aspect of discipled thinking that is crucial for spiritual growth.

If your mind is a garden, **this is your planting list:**
- Truth
- Honor
- Justice
- Purity
- Beauty
- Excellence
- Praise

You must pull like a weed—every thought that doesn't align with **these things.**

Replace your thoughts using the spiritual discipline of meditation—not emptying your mind but filling it with divine truth.

You don't overcome negative thoughts by "trying not to think about them." You overcome by **replacing them** with better ones.

SECTION 5. **Building a Truth-Based Thought Life**

Stewardship of the mind isn't a one-time decision—it's a **daily discipline.**

Here's how to build a truth-based thought life:

1. **Renewal Routine**
   Start each day with a Scripture that aligns with your area of need for a breakthrough. Say it out loud, meditate on it, and let it frame your mindset.

2. **Thought Audit**
   Once a week, write down recurring thoughts you've been entertaining. These could be thoughts of self-doubt, fear, or negativity. Ask: Is this true? Is it biblical? Is it helpful? If not, replace it with a more positive and truthful thought.

3. **Declare and Replace**
   When toxic thoughts appear, declare the truth immediately. Train your mind to respond in faith, not fear.

4. **Mental Margin**
   Take time each day without the noise—no phone, no media. Let your mind breathe. Clarity thrives in silence.

5. **Accountability**
   Invite someone to challenge your thinking. Let them ask you, "Is that what God says about you?"

You cannot steward your calling if you're a prisoner of your thoughts. So, choose daily: *Will I partner with truth or tolerate lies?*

SECTION 6. **Reflection Questions**

1. What thought patterns have been shaping my life without permission?
2. What lies have I accepted that contradict God's Word?

3. How can I begin renewing my mind daily?
4. Who can help hold me accountable to steward my thought life?

SECTION 7. **Prayer Declaration**

Father, thank You for the gift of my mind. I surrender every thought, belief, and mental pattern to You. I cast down lies and raise the truth. Teach me to think like You—Fill my mind with peace, clarity, and faith. I align my thoughts with Your Kingdom and walk in renewed strength. In Jesus' name, amen.

Chapter 2.2

God's Thoughts

Scripture Focus:
Isaiah 55:8–9, 1 Corinthians 2:16, Psalm 139:17–18

Isaiah 55:8-9 (KJV) *8 For my thoughts are not your thoughts, neither are your ways my ways, saith the LORD. 9 For as the heavens are higher than the earth, so are my ways higher than your ways, and my thoughts than your thoughts.*

1 Corinthians 2:16 (KJV) *16 For who hath known the mind of the Lord, that he may instruct him? But we have the mind of Christ.*

Psalms 139:17-18 (KJV) *17 How precious also are thy thoughts unto me, O God! how great is the sum of them! 18 If I should count them, they are more in number than the sand: when I awake, I am still with thee.*

INTRODUCTION. Learning to Think Like God

One of the greatest privileges of walking with God is the invitation to **think like Him.**

> *"For My thoughts are not your thoughts, neither are your ways My ways," declares the Lord.* — Isaiah 55:8

At first glance, this sounds like a rejection. But in truth, it's an invitation. God isn't saying, *"You'll never understand Me."* He's saying, *"Your natural thoughts can't reach Me—but I want to lift yours to Mine."*

"We have the mind of Christ." — 1 Corinthians 2:16

The mind of Christ means:
- You can adopt the Kingdom's perspective

- You can download wisdom in real-time
- You can process situations through God's lens
- You can think, plan, and lead with divine insight

This chapter will help you:
- Identify when your thoughts oppose God's
- Align your mindset with His Word
- Develop a lifestyle of thinking in sync with the Kingdom

God's thoughts are not just higher—they're holier, wiser, and more effective—and He wants to share them with you.

SECTION 1. Isaiah 55—The Elevation of Divine Thought

"For My thoughts are not your thoughts, neither are your ways My ways," declares the Lord. "As the heavens are higher than the earth, so are My ways higher than your ways..." — Isaiah 55:8–9

This Scripture is one of the most quoted and one of the most misunderstood Scriptures about God's thoughts.

God is not rubbing our face in how inferior we are. He's **inviting us to upgrade** our mindset.

When He says His thoughts are higher, He means:
- They're redemptive, not reactive
- They see the entire story, not just the current struggle
- They are rooted in truth, not trauma
- They are eternally focused, not emotionally driven

To steward your life well, you need access to the Kingdom's point of view.

God doesn't just want you to behave better—He wants you to **believe differently.** That means letting His Word challenge your assumptions, disrupt your doubts, and reframe your conclusions.

Wherever your thoughts contradict His thoughts, you have a choice:
- *Do I cling to my perspective or surrender to His?*
- You can't walk in divine results while living by natural reasoning.

SECTION 2. 1 Corinthians 2—The Mind of Christ

"But we have the mind of Christ." — 1 Corinthians 2:16

Let this profound truth sink in: God not only wants you to believe in Jesus but also to **think like Him.**

That means:
- You can access God's wisdom in your decisions
- You can discern the spiritual truth behind natural problems
- You can respond in faith when others panic in fear
- You can approach leadership with a supernatural strategy

The mind of Christ isn't about IQ—it's about intimacy.

As you spend time in prayer, the Word, worship, and wise community, your thinking **shifts.** You stop jumping to conclusions. You start seeking God's counsel first. You stop reacting to fear. You start responding from peace.

The mind of Christ becomes your internal compass. It keeps you centered in storms, grounded in conflict, and focused in chaos.

SECTION 3. Replacing My Thoughts with His

Alignment doesn't happen automatically; it requires intentional replacement. You cannot adopt God's thoughts while clinging to your own. Something must go.

"Let the wicked forsake their ways and the unrighteous their thoughts..." — Isaiah 55:7

Transformation starts where surrender begins.
This is how you replace your thoughts with God's:

1. **Identify the Conflict**
   What am I thinking that doesn't align with His Word?
   Example:
   - My thought: *"I'm always overlooked."*
   - God's thought: *"You are chosen and appointed."* — John 15:16

2. **Find the Truth**
   What scripture directly challenges that thought?

   Example: "I'll never recover from this." Truth: "He restores my soul."
   — Psalm 23:3

3. **Declare Until It Dominates**
   Speak the truth out loud. Daily. Truth doesn't set you free until it **becomes your new normal.**
   Renewing your mind means **not just believing the truth but thinking it intentionally.**

SECTION 4. How to Discern When a Thought Isn't from God

Not every thought that feels urgent is from the Kingdom. Here's how to test it:

Ask yourself:
- Is it rooted in fear or faith?
- Does it align with Scripture?
- Does it accuse or affirm my identity in Christ?
- Does it lead me to peace or panic?
- Would Jesus say this to me?

If the answer to any of those questions exposes contradiction, **don't entertain the thought; evict it immediately.**

God's voice corrects and convicts but never condemns. God's thoughts will stretch you, not strangle you. God's ideas bring clarity, not confusion.

If the thought doesn't bear God's fingerprints, it's not from Him.

SECTION 5. Practicing God-Aligned Thinking

Thinking like God is not just a belief; it's a **daily practice.** You train your brain to align with the truth the same way you train your body to grow strong: repetition, resistance, and rest.

Here are five practical ways to cultivate God-aligned thinking:

1. **Truth Journaling**
   Each day, write down one thought that tried to dominate your mind. Underneath it, write a scripture that confronts it.
2. **Declare the Upgrade**
   Find three scriptures that reflect God's thoughts about you or your situation. Speak them aloud in the morning and before bed.
3. **Think in Praise**
   When tempted to spiral, stop and say: *"Lord, I praise You for what You're doing even if I don't see it yet."*
   Praise redirects your thoughts from problems to promises.
4. **Mental Mentors**
   Surround yourself with thinkers who elevate your faith. Podcasts, books, conversations—all influence your thought life.
5. **Ask Daily: "Is This What God Thinks?"**
   Make it a habit. Train yourself to pause before partnering with a thought. The Holy Spirit will reveal what you need to replace.

God's thoughts are available—but only to those willing to replace their own.

SECTION 6. Reflection Questions

1. What recurring thoughts do I entertain that contradict God's Word?
2. What truths from Scripture do I need to declare over my life daily?
3. How can I recognize the difference between my thoughts and God's?
4. What can I do this week to begin thinking more like Christ?

SECTION 7. Prayer Declaration

Father, thank You for inviting me to think like You. I repent for entertaining thoughts that don't reflect Your truth. I surrender my mindset to You. Help me see what You see, believe what You say, and think like the Kingdom. I declare that I have the mind of Christ. My thoughts are holy, clear, and filled with faith. In Jesus' name, amen.

Chapter 2.3

The Knowledge That Builds

Scripture Focus:
Hosea 4:6, Proverbs 24:3–5, Colossians 1:9–10, 2 Peter 1:5–8

Hosea 4:6 (KJV) *6 My people are destroyed for lack of knowledge: because thou hast rejected knowledge, I will also reject thee, that thou shalt be no priest to me: seeing thou hast forgotten the law of thy God, I will also forget thy children.*

Proverbs 24:3-5 (KJV) *3 Through wisdom is an house builded; and by understanding it is established: 4 And by knowledge shall the chambers be filled with all precious and pleasant riches. 5 A wise man is strong; yea, a man of knowledge increaseth strength.*

Colossians 1:9-10 (KJV) *9 For this cause we also, since the day we heard it, do not cease to pray for you, and to desire that ye might be filled with the knowledge of his will in all wisdom and spiritual understanding; 10 That ye might walk worthy of the Lord unto all pleasing, being fruitful in every good work, and increasing in the knowledge of God;*

2 Peter 1:5-8 (KJV) *5 And beside this, giving all diligence, add to your faith virtue; and to virtue knowledge; 6 And to knowledge temperance; and to temperance patience; and to patience godliness; 7 And to godliness brotherly kindness; and to brotherly kindness charity. 8 For if these things be in you, and abound, they make you that ye shall neither be barren nor unfruitful in the knowledge of our Lord Jesus Christ*

INTRODUCTION. Not All Knowledge is Created Equal

We live in an age overflowing with information, yet we are starving for transformation.

Podcasts, articles, sermons, books, videos, they're everywhere. But **not all knowledge builds.** Some knowledge distracts. Some knowledge puffs up. Some knowledge even deceives.

"My people are destroyed for lack of knowledge..." — Hosea 4:6

God isn't warning about academic ignorance—He's talking about **spiritual negligence.** When we stop pursuing divine knowledge, our stewardship suffers. When we lack stewardship, we misuse time, mismanage people, and misplace purpose.

But there is a kind of knowledge that:
- Builds character
- Builds faith
- Builds businesses
- Builds families
- Builds Kingdom legacy from the Kingdom's perspective

This chapter is about that kind of knowledge. A knowledge that bears fruit, aligns with truth, and empowers wise action.

Because what you **know** determines what you can **build.**

SECTION 1. Hosea 4—Destroyed by What You Don't Know

"My people are destroyed for lack of knowledge..." — Hosea 4:6

Knowledge isn't just about knowing facts; it's about knowing God. Israel's destruction wasn't because they lacked resources; it was because they abandoned **revelation.**

When you cease to nourish your mind with truth, destruction begins to seep in by default. Truth serves as a shield against destruction, underscoring the vital importance of knowing God's Word in our lives.

Ignorance is not a state of innocence; it's a state of vulnerability. It serves as a reminder of the role of knowledge in protecting us from harm and guiding us on our life's journey.

Many believers fail in their finances, relationships, leadership, or ministry not because of rebellion but because of a **lack of knowledge.**

You don't rise to the level of your intention—**you rise to the level of your instruction.**

And if you're not growing in godly knowledge, you're stuck in cycles of confusion and delay.
- You'll repeat what you don't understand.
- You'll tolerate what you don't discern.
- You'll miss opportunities you're not trained to steward.

That's why growth in knowledge begins with **humility**: "Lord, teach me what I don't know."

SECTION 2. Proverbs 24—Knowledge Fills the House

"By wisdom a house is built, and through understanding it is established; through knowledge its rooms are filled with rare and beautiful treasures." — Proverbs 24:3-4

Look at the divine sequence:
- Wisdom **builds**
- Understanding **strengthens**
- Knowledge **fills**

You can build a structure, but without knowledge, it stays empty. In your life, knowledge fills the rooms with:
- Financial stewardship
- Communication skills
- Emotional intelligence
- Biblical literacy
- Entrepreneurial discipline
- Parenting insight
- Relational discernment

The more you know, the more God can flow. Not so you can boast, but so you can build.

The benefit of knowledge is why stewards are constant learners. You cannot carry tomorrow's assignment with yesterday's understanding.

SECTION 3. Colossians 1—Knowledge That Leads to Fruit

> "...that you may be filled with the knowledge of His will in all wisdom and spiritual understanding; that you may walk worthy of the Lord... being fruitful in every good work..." — Colossians 1:9–10

Paul's prayer wasn't just about seeking information. It was a quest for spiritual understanding, a key element in bearing fruit.

Understanding is the kind of knowledge that:
- Clarifies direction
- Strengthens conviction
- Aligns daily decisions with eternal outcomes
- Produces real, measurable fruit

Notice the progression:
- Be filled with knowledge
- Gain wisdom and spiritual understanding
- Walk in a way that pleases God
- Produce fruit in every good work

The true goal of knowledge is not simply to accumulate more facts but to use that knowledge to make better decisions and take more effective actions. **In other words, the goal is not merely to know more but to do better.**

The most educated person in the room is not the one who talks the most. It's the one who bears the most fruit in obedience.

SECTION 4. 2 Peter 1—Add to Your Faith Knowledge

> "...make every effort to add to your faith goodness; and to goodness, knowledge..." — 2 Peter 1:5

Faith is your foundation, but knowledge is part of your structure. **You must add goodness and knowledge to your faith.**

Too many believers stop at salvation. They believe in Jesus but never grow in their understanding and practice of His teachings. They're sincere but underdeveloped.

Peter says: "Make every effort." In other words, **knowledge won't come passively.**

You must:
- Read
- Study
- Ask
- Observe
- Practice
- Learn from correction
- Learn from others

Spiritual maturity requires **mental discipline.** You can't outsource your growth. You must become a student of the Word, of your assignment (your unique role or purpose in God's plan), and wisdom.

A teachable spirit is a fruitful spirit.

SECTION 5. Practical Knowledge-Building Disciplines

Faithful stewards never stop learning. Here are five practical ways to grow in the knowledge that builds:

1. **Daily Wisdom Intake**
   Immerse yourself in the transformative power of Scripture. Start your day by reading at least one chapter of Proverbs or Psalms. These books are not just words on a page; they are tools that train the heart and sharpen the mind.

2. **Topical Bible Study**
   Pick one area of life you need to grow in (leadership, money, relationships, purpose). Search Scripture and build understanding on that topic.

3. **Skill Stacking**
   Identify two or three skills that support your calling. Take online courses, read books, or find mentors to grow faster and wiser.

4. **Mentor Moments**
   Ask questions often. Seek out people who are doing what you desire to do and take notes. What took them ten years can take you ten months if you learn from them.
5. **Teach What You Learn**
   Teaching solidifies learning. Share what God is teaching you in a small group, video, or journal. When you can teach it, you own it.

SECTION 6. Reflection Questions

1. What areas of my life are suffering due to a lack of knowledge?
2. Where am I growing in information but not bearing fruit?
3. What knowledge do I need to pursue in this season to build wisely?
4. Who are three mentors or resources I can pursue for growth?

SECTION 7. Prayer Declaration

Father, thank You for the truth that builds. I ask for hunger to grow in the knowledge of Your will. Help me steward what I know and seek what I lack. I declare that I am not lazy; I am teachable. I am not stagnant; I am growing. My mind is sharp, my spirit is willing, and my life is fruitful. In Jesus' name, amen.

KEY THREE

CONFESSION

(What You Say)

Chapter 3.1

The Power of Words

Scripture Focus:
Proverbs 18:21, James 3:3–6, Matthew 12:36–37

Proverbs 18:2 (KJV) *21 Death and life are in the power of the tongue: and they that love it shall eat the fruit thereof.*

James 3:3-6 (KJV) *3 Behold, we put bits in the horses' mouths, that they may obey us; and we turn about their whole body. 4 Behold also the ships, which though they be so great, and are driven of fierce winds, yet are they turned about with a very small helm, whithersoever the governor listeth. 5 Even so the tongue is a little member, and boasteth great things. Behold, how great a matter a little fire kindleth! 6 And the tongue is a fire, a world of iniquity: so is the tongue among our members, that it defileth the whole body, and setteth on fire the course of nature; and it is set on fire of hell.*

Matthew 12:36-37 (KJV) *36 But I say unto you, That every idle word that men shall speak, they shall give account thereof in the day of judgment. 37 For by thy words thou shalt be justified, and by thy words thou shalt be condemned.*

INTRODUCTION. Words Create Worlds

Your words are not just sounds—they are seeds. They carry power, authority, and the ability to shape environments, relationships, destinies, and even nations.

"Death and life are in the power of the tongue..." — Proverbs 18:21

That's not poetry. It's a spiritual law. God created the universe with words, and as His image-bearers, so do we.
- Words frame what we believe.
- Words reveal what's hidden in our hearts.
- Words unlock or delay purpose.
- Words establish a spiritual atmosphere in our homes, churches, and businesses.

In the Kingdom, what you say can:
- Heal or hurt
- Open or close doors
- Bless or curse
- Advance or sabotage your stewardship

Your confession is a form of construction. You're either building with bricks of truth or with blocks of fear, sarcasm, and doubt.

This chapter will help you:
- Understand the authority of your voice
- Guard your mouth with discernment
- Start speaking life that aligns with the Kingdom

Because what you say consistently is what you will eventually see.

SECTION 1. **Proverbs 18—The Tongue Has Power**

"Death and life are in the power of the tongue, and those who love it will eat its fruit." — Proverbs 18:21

The tongue is not neutral—it's a weapon. You have the power to speak life or death into a situation. And Scripture says **you'll eat the fruit of what you plant.** This means you have the responsibility and the power to shape your reality with your words. That means:
- Speak fear, and you'll live anxiously.
- Speak bitterness, and you'll dwell in offense.
- Speak doubt, and you'll shrink from opportunity.
- Speak belief, and you'll attract favor.
- Speak peace, and you'll establish order.
- Speak faith and blessings, and you'll shift generations.

Your mouth is a multiplier. It takes what's inside you and releases it into the atmosphere around you. Your words have the potential to transform the environment, for better or for worse. This is the weight of your speech.

Stewardship of the tongue is essential for Kingdom leadership. If God has trusted you with people, platforms, or purpose, then what you say is not casual—it's catalytic.

So, what are you consistently saying over:
- Your family?
- Your finances?
- Your future?
- Your business or ministry?

If it doesn't sound like something the Kingdom would say, it shouldn't live in your mouth.

SECTION 2. James 3—Taming What Drives the Direction

> *"The tongue is a small part of the body, but it makes great boasts. Consider what a great forest is set on fire by a small spark..."* — James 3:5

James compares the tongue to three things:
- A bit in a horse's mouth
- A rudder on a ship
- A spark that starts a wildfire

Each example illustrates that **something small can have a significant impact on something big.**
- A small bit directs a 1,500-pound horse.
- A tiny rudder directs a massive ship.
- A single spark can destroy entire forests.

And so is your life.

Your tongue sets the course, and you hold the reins. You can pray, plan, and pursue, but if your words are out of alignment, your direction will follow your declaration.

Many people are unknowingly shaping their present and future with their self-talk, often laced with passive sarcasm and casual pessimism. They may not realize it, but they're authorizing outcomes they never desired.

"I'll never get out of this." "I always mess up." "Things never work for me."

These aren't just phrases—they're **prophetic permissions, spoken by choice.** You're steering your ship straight into storms you are to avoid, but you have the power to change that.

SECTION 3. Jesus on Words—Accountable and Authorized

> *"But I tell you that everyone will have to give account on the day of judgment for every empty word they have spoken. For by your words you will be acquitted, and by your words you will be condemned."* — Matthew 12:36–37

Jesus didn't say you'd be judged by your actions alone. He said **your words** carry weight in the courtroom of Heaven.

Words are not background noise in the spirit; they are evidence. Receipts. They prove what you believe, what you value, and what you fear.

This Scripture isn't about fear of judgment alone; it's about **stewardship of influence.** When you speak the Word of God, **things move:**
- Angels respond (Psalm 103:20)
- Demons retreat (Luke 10:19)
- Faith builds (Romans 10:17)
- Atmospheres shift (Acts 16:25–26)

Speak in line with the Kingdom, and you **release divine activity.** But when you complain, curse, or slander, you empower the enemy. It's a responsibility and power that we must all be mindful of.

Every word either creates or contaminates. It's a sobering thought, but it's the truth.

So, Jesus advises, Be mindful of your speech. Why? Because your words are keys. They can either open or close the door to what God wants to do through you.

SECTION 4. The Echo of the Heart

"Out of the abundance of the heart the mouth speaks." — Matthew 12:34

Your mouth is a mirror. It shows what's overflowing in your heart. If you want to know what's going on inside you:
- Listen to your language under pressure
- Watch what you say when you're tired
- Track how you speak about yourself, your family, and your future

Your confession reveals your meditation. You can't fake it for long. Eventually, **your mouth will echo your mindset.**

The power in your confession is **why stewardship of words** (which means taking responsibility for the words you use) **requires stewardship of the heart.** You don't just fix your mouth; you fix your motives. You heal your heart. You renew your mind.

With this understanding, your words will naturally begin to shift.

SECTION 5. How to Start Speaking Like a Steward

Words are not just tools; they are powerful instruments that can shape your reality. The more skilled you are with them, the more Kingdom authority you carry. Here are five ways to speak like a steward:

1. **Speak the Word, Not Just Feelings**
   Base your confessions on Scripture. Feelings fluctuate; truth stands firm. Example: Instead of "I'm scared," say, "God has not given me a spirit of fear..." (2 Tim 1:7)
2. **Speak Life into Dead Places**
   Even if you see no fruit, prophesy the promise. God told Ezekiel to speak to dry bones. Why? Because faith speaks before it sees.
3. **Create a Confession Habit**
   Each morning or evening, declare 3–5 affirmations/confessions based on God's promises over your life, family, purpose, and provision.

4. **Cancel Negative Agreements**
   If you catch yourself saying something toxic, say out loud, "I cancel that in Jesus' name. I align my words with the Kingdom."
5. **Bless, Don't Curse**
   That includes yourself, your leaders, your spouse, your kids, and even your enemies. Why? Because blessing releases freedom, and stewardship begins with honor.

SECTION 6. Reflection Questions

1. What am I consistently saying about my life, family, or calling?
2. Do my words align more with fear or with faith?
3. Who or what have I unknowingly cursed with careless speech?
4. What three confessions should I begin declaring daily?

SECTION 7. Prayer Declaration

Father, I repent for every word I've spoken that didn't reflect Your truth. I surrender my tongue to You. Teach me how to communicate with faith, clarity, and blessing. Help me to align my words with Your will. I declare my mouth is a wellspring of life. I speak only what builds, heals, and advances Your Kingdom. In Jesus' name, amen.

Chapter 3.2

Confessions Create Culture

Scripture Focus:
Genesis 1:3, Proverbs 15:4, Psalm 19:14, Titus 2:7–8

Genesis 1:3 (KJV) *3 And God said, Let there be light: and there was light.*

Proverbs 15:4 (KJV) *4 A wholesome tongue is a tree of life: but perverseness therein is a breach in the spirit.*

Psalms 19:14 (KJV) *14 Let the words of my mouth, and the meditation of my heart, be acceptable in thy sight, O LORD, my strength, and my redeemer.*

Titus 2:7-8 (KJV) *7 In all things shewing thyself a pattern of good works: in doctrine shewing uncorruptness, gravity, sincerity, 8 Sound speech, that cannot be condemned; that he that is of the contrary part may be ashamed, having no evil thing to say of you.*

INTRODUCTION. Atmospheres Are Spoken Before They're Built

Vision statements or slogans communicate intentions, but it's the words we speak daily that create and transform the culture. Every culture is built and transformed **word by word**, moment by moment, and conversation by conversation.

> *"And God said, 'Let there be light,' and there was light."* — Genesis 1:3

God didn't build creation with His hands; He built it with **His mouth.** He spoke, and **the atmosphere obeyed.**

As His image-bearers, we carry the responsibility of shaping the atmosphere around us with our words. Our words have the power to build or destroy, to create or dismantle. It's up to us to use this power wisely.

In our:
- Home
- Marriage
- Ministry
- Business
- Team
- Church

The culture we experience is the culture in which our words play a significant role in creating.

If people feel at peace, experience clarity, and receive encouragement in your presence, it's because your confession consistently plants those seeds. If people feel tension, fear, or uncertainty, it's likely your words are contributing to it.

This chapter will help you:
- Understand how confession builds an emotional and spiritual atmosphere
- Identify cultural patterns created by careless speech
- Intentionally craft environments that reflect Kingdom values

Because every steward is also a **culture carrier,** and culture is carried through words.

SECTION 1. **What You Say Sets the Tone**

Every room you enter, every call you lead, every home you live in, you are setting the **tone** with your words.

> "A gentle tongue is a tree of life, but perverseness in it breaks the spirit." — Proverbs 15:4

Remember, your tone doesn't start with volume; it begins with **intention.** You have the power to set the tone in every interaction.
- Are you speaking to build up or break down?
- Are you speaking to inspire or to impress?
- Are your words healing or harming?

Whether you're leading a church or raising a child, your voice becomes a soundtrack. People begin to hear your language **even when you're not present.**

Your consistent confession becomes the cultural expectation.
Example:
- If you always say, *"We get through tough seasons together,"* your team learns resilience.
- If you say, *"We don't speak badly about people who aren't in the room,"* you build honor.
- If you say, *"We expect excellence, but we give grace,"* you form a culture of both growth and safety.

Remember, what you repeat becomes what people remember and eventually replicate. Your words and actions carry weight.

SECTION 2. How Confession Affects Environments

Words are not mere descriptors of culture; they are the architects that shape it. In other words, **words don't just describe culture; they decide it.**

> *"Let the words of my mouth and the meditation of my heart be acceptable in Your sight…"* — Psalm 19:14

Why did David offer this prayer? Because he recognized the spiritual potency of words as builders of our reality.

In your home:
- Speak peace, and peace increases.
- Speak chaos and confusion multiplies.

In your team:
- Speak vision, and energy grows.
- Speak negativity, and progress slows.

In your church:
- Speak honor, and unity strengthens.
- Speak criticism, and division creeps in.

Jesus knew the power of words and was intentional with His language:
- He **called Simon "Peter"** before he acted like a rock.
- He **called Jairus's daughter "not dead"** before she breathed again.

- He **spoke to a storm** before it ceased.
- He **spoke to a tree** before it dried up.
- He **blessed the bread** before it multiplied.

Culture follows confession. What you speak consistently begins to grow.

SECTION 3. The Language of Honor and Hope

If you want to shift culture, shift your **language. Honor and hope** are two of the most potent cultural forces you can release with your mouth.

> *"In your teaching show integrity, seriousness, and soundness of speech that cannot be condemned..."* — Titus 2:7–8

Honor Speaks to Value

To honor someone is to recognize God's hand on them, even when they're imperfect. Honor says, *"I see who God made you to be, and I'll treat you accordingly."*

When you speak honorably:
- Correction lands with grace, not shame
- Team members feel safe to grow
- Authority is received, not resisted

In families, honor is about acknowledging identity in your children, *not just correcting behavior but affirming destiny.*

In churches, honor is demonstrated by affirming leaders publicly, correcting them privately, and refraining from making jokes at the expense of someone's worth.

Honor isn't flattery. Flattery is insincere praise given to manipulate or gain favor. Honor, on the other hand, is genuine respect and recognition of someone's worth. **It's spiritual reinforcement** that builds people up and strengthens relationships.

Hope Speaks to the Future

Hope-filled language isn't naive—it's **prophetic.** It doesn't deny challenges, but it speaks of what **God is doing despite them.**

When you consistently say things like:
- "God's not done with us yet."
- "There's more on the other side of this."
- "We've seen Him move before, and we'll see it again."

You build a **culture of resilience**. Hope keeps people moving. Honor keeps them united.

SECTION 4. Culture-Killing Confessions to Avoid

Specific phrases poison culture over time. Even if they sound casual, they train people to expect negativity. Watch out for:
- "That's just how I am." *(rejects accountability)*
- "We've tried that before—it won't work." *(kills innovation)*
- "People just don't care anymore." *(breeds cynicism)*
- "They're not ready for this." *(sows division)*
- "I guess it is what it is." *(silences faith)*

Remember, you have the power to change the narrative. You may think you're venting, but you might be **inviting dysfunction to stay.**

Confession isn't just about theology; it's about tone-setting. **The wrong phrases create ceilings. The right ones open windows.**

SECTION 5. Building a Kingdom Culture with Words

Every culture builder in Scripture wielded the power of intentional speech. Moses, with his speeches, shaped generations. Nehemiah, through bold declarations, inspired a rebuilding crew. Jesus, beyond mere preaching, used his words to **form** Kingdom culture.

You, too, have the power to follow in their footsteps.

Here are five ways to build a Kingdom culture through confession:

1. **Establish Verbal Values**
   Choose 3–5 phrases that embody the essence of your home, business, or ministry. These are not just words; they are the pillars of your culture. Repeat them often to reinforce their importance.
   Here are a few examples:
   - "We do excellence with humility."

- "We speak what we want to see."
- "We correct with grace and truth."

2. **Outlaw Toxic Talk**
   Draw a hard line on gossip, sarcasm, and cynicism. Culture dies when you allow toxicity.

3. **Speak Identity Over People**
   Tell your spouse, kids, team members: "You are anointed. You are wise. You're a builder. God's hand is on you." **Say it before they believe it. Say it until they see it.**

4. **Prophesy Progress**
   Even when you're not there yet, say: *"We're growing. We're healing. We're gaining ground."*

5. **Echo Heaven**
   Ask: *"What does God say about this space?"* Then, align your speech accordingly. Let every environment reflect Kingdom clarity.

When your confession aligns with the Kingdom, the culture around you begins to shift on earth.

SECTION 6. Reflection Questions

1. What is the atmosphere my words are creating at home, work, or church?
2. What repeated phrases have unintentionally damaged the culture around me?
3. What values do I need to speak more often?
4. How can I begin using words to reflect honor and hope?

SECTION 7. Prayer Declaration

Father, thank You for entrusting me with influence. I surrender my speech to You. Teach me to use my words to build a culture that honors You. Fill my mouth with wisdom, kindness, clarity, and truth. May every environment I enter shift toward the Kingdom because of what I say. I declare that I am a culture carrier—called, equipped, and entrusted to speak life. In Jesus' name, amen.

Chapter 3.3

Declaring What God Said

Scripture Focus:
Ezekiel 37:1–10, Isaiah 55:11, Hebrews 10:23, Mark 11:23

Ezekiel 37:1-10 (KJV) *1 The hand of the LORD was upon me, and carried me out in the spirit of the LORD, and set me down in the midst of the valley which was full of bones, 2 And caused me to pass by them round about: and, behold, there were very many in the open valley; and, lo, they were very dry. 3 And he said unto me, Son of man, can these bones live? And I answered, O Lord GOD, thou knowest. 4 Again he said unto me, Prophesy upon these bones, and say unto them, O ye dry bones, hear the word of the LORD. 5 Thus saith the Lord GOD unto these bones; Behold, I will cause breath to enter into you, and ye shall live: 6 And I will lay sinews upon you, and will bring up flesh upon you, and cover you with skin, and put breath in you, and ye shall live; and ye shall know that I am the LORD. 7 So I prophesied as I was commanded: and as I prophesied, there was a noise, and behold a shaking, and the bones came together, bone to his bone. 8 And when I beheld, lo, the sinews and the flesh came up upon them, and the skin covered them above: but there was no breath in them. 9 Then said he unto me, Prophesy unto the wind, prophesy, son of man, and say to the wind, Thus saith the Lord GOD; Come from the four winds, O breath, and breathe upon these slain, that they may live. 10 So I prophesied as he commanded me, and the breath came into them, and they lived, and stood up upon their feet, an exceeding great army.*

Isaiah 55:11 (KJV) *11 So shall my word be that goeth forth out of my mouth: it shall not return unto me void, but* it shall accomplish that which I please, and it shall prosper in the thing whereto I sent it.

Hebrews 10:23 (KJV) *23 Let us hold fast the profession of our faith without wavering; (for he is faithful that promised;)*

Mark 11:23 (KJV) *23 For verily I say unto you, That whosoever shall say unto this mountain, Be thou removed, and be thou cast into the sea; and shall not doubt in his heart, but shall believe that those things which he saith shall come to pass; he shall have whatsoever he saith.*

INTRODUCTION. Speak What God Has Spoken

The highest use of your voice is not to express opinions—it's to **echo The Kingdom.**

> *"Let the redeemed of the Lord say so…"* — Psalm 107:2

God expects His redeemed people to **repeat what He has revealed.**
In a world filled with opinions, arguments, and emotions, a steward must ask:
- What has **God said** about this?
- Am I **saying what He said,** or just reacting to what I see?

Confession isn't about making something up. It's about coming into **agreement with what already exists in God's Kingdom.**
- He says, "You are healed," meaning He has already healed you.
- He says you are the head and not the tail.
- He says you are more than a conqueror.
- He says His Word will not return void.

When your mouth matches His Word, **miracles begin to manifest.**
This chapter will help you:
- Speak with Kingdom authority
- Align your words with Scripture
- See dry places come to life through prophetic declaration

SECTION 1. Ezekiel 37—Prophesy to Dry Bones

"Then He said to me, 'Prophesy to these bones and say to them...'" — Ezekiel 37:4

God placed Ezekiel in a valley full of dry bones that were lifeless, hopeless, and scattered, then gave him a strange command: **speak**.

God could have brought the bones to life with a thought. But He chose to do it through a man's **mouth**.

Why? Because God made Man in His image and after His likeness, then gave him dominion over all the Earth (Gen 1:26-28). So, when God wants to accomplish something on Earth, He chooses the method of partnership.

He asks: *"Can these bones live?"* And when Ezekiel defers, God says: *"Prophesy to them."*

Your voice carries God's permission. Your declaration awakens dormant purpose. What you **say in faith** can resurrect what seems dead.

When Ezekiel obeyed, the bones came together and formed bodies; then, after being filled with breath, an army stood up.

A prophetic declaration is not wishful thinking—it's speaking what God has already willed. In your own "valleys," God may be waiting for you to stop narrating the dryness and start **speaking life**.

SECTION 2. Isaiah 55—God's Word Will Not Return Void

"So is My word that goes out from My mouth: it will not return to Me empty..." — Isaiah 55:11

God's Word is **seed and sword**, and it never fails.
But here's the key: It must be **sent**.
When God speaks, Heaven moves. But when **you** speak what God says, **Heaven partners with Earth**.

That means:
- When you speak healing, God backs it.
- When you declare provision, angels are dispatched.
- When you proclaim truth, darkness is pushed back.

God's Word always works, but it must be **released.**

When His Word fills your heart and comes out of your mouth, your confession becomes a **conduit for power.**

SECTION 3. Mark 11—Say to the Mountain

"Truly I tell you, if anyone says to this mountain, 'Go, throw yourself into the sea,' and does not doubt... it will be done for them." — Mark 11:23

Jesus didn't say, *"Think about the mountain."* He didn't say, *"Complain about the mountain."* He said, **"Speak to it."**

Mountains in Scripture represent obstacles, strongholds, and impossible odds. And Jesus says they don't move by effort; they move by the power of your faith-filled confession.

You have the power to move your mountains.

What are you speaking to?

- Are you rehearsing the problem or **releasing authority**?
- Are you describing the issue or **declaring the outcome**?

Faith has a voice, and silence isn't neutral. If you're not speaking the Word, you're leaving space for fear and doubt to speak for you.

You don't need perfect grammar. You don't need a preacher's voice. What you need is faith, which is a confident belief in the truth of God's promises and a willingness to agree with those promises. This means aligning your thoughts, words, and actions with what God has said about your situation.

Speak to your finances. Speak to your body. Speak to your children. Speak to your business. Speak to your purpose.

Remember, mountains still move, but only if you **command them to.** Your faith-filled confessions have the power to transform your circumstances, so speak with authority and believe in God's promises.

SECTION 4. How to Declare God's Word Daily

Declaring what God has said isn't complicated; it's consistent. Here's how to make it a part of your daily life:

1. **Build a Declaration List**

   Write 10–15 Scriptures that speak to your identity, purpose, provision, peace, and promise. Declare them each morning.

2. **Declare During Warfare**
   When you're under pressure or confusion, **don't just think—speak.** The Word spoken becomes a sword.

3. **Use Scripture in Prayer**
   Pray the Word. Insert God's promises into your intercession:
   - "Father, You said I am the head and not the tail..."
   - "Your Word says You will supply all my needs..."

4. **Teach Your Family to Declare**
   Let your spouse, kids, or team hear faith on your lips. Model what it looks like to **stand on the Word out loud.**
   Confession creates alignment. Alignment releases power.

SECTION 5. Shifting Outcomes Through Confession

There are moments when strategy won't shift your situation, but **confession will.**

Some breakthroughs don't require more work; they need more **Word.**

Here's what making a declaration does:
- **It aligns your soul with God's perspective**
- **It builds faith in the unseen**
- **It activates angelic assignment** (Psalm 103:20)
- **It silences the lies of the enemy**
- **It sows seeds into your future** that bring a harvest in due time

Don't underestimate what happens when you open your mouth with conviction. Dry bones become armies. Mountains dive into oceans. Darkness lifts. Delay breaks—and the Kingdom gets involved.

You may not see it immediately, but every time you declare God's Word, you're persistently building, brick by brick.
- You're building peace.
- You're building courage.
- You're building your house on the rock.

Don't just **read** the Bible—**speak it.** Declare verses that speak to your situation, such as 'I can do all things through Christ who strengthens me' (Philippians 4:13) or 'The Lord is my shepherd, I shall not want' (Psalm 23:1).

Because God's Word in your mouth is just as powerful as it is in His **when spoken by faith,** which is unwavering belief and trust in its truth and power.

SECTION 6. Reflection Questions

1. What has God said about my current situation that I haven't been declaring?
2. Where have I been silent when I should be speaking?
3. What Scriptures do I need to memorize and declare daily?
4. What "mountains" am I tolerating instead of commanding?

SECTION 7. Prayer Declaration

Father, I thank You for Your Word. I repent for every time I've spoken doubt or stayed silent when I should've spoken the truth. I align my confession with Your promises. Let Your Word rise in me like fire. I declare life over every dry place. I speak to every mountain and say, "Move." I prophesy to my purpose, my family, and my future. I declare what You have said, and I expect to see what You've spoken. In Jesus' name, amen. the

KEY FOUR

WORK AND WISDOM

(What You Do)

Chapter 4.1

The Wisdom to Work It

Scripture Focus:
Proverbs 24:3–4, James 1:5, Colossians 3:23, Ecclesiastes 10:10

Proverbs 24:3-4 (KJV) *3 Through wisdom is an house builded; and by understanding it is established: 4 And by knowledge shall the chambers be filled with all precious and pleasant riches.*

James 1:5 (KJV) *5 If any of you lack wisdom, let him ask of God, that giveth to all men liberally, and upbraideth not; and it shall be given him.*

Colossians 3:23 (KJV) *23 And whatsoever ye do, do it heartily, as to the Lord, and not unto men;*

Ecclesiastes 10:10 (KJV) *10 If the iron be blunt, and he do not whet the edge, then must he put to more strength: but wisdom is profitable to direct.*

INTRODUCTION. When Vision Meets Wisdom and Work

You can have the most incredible vision in the world, but if you lack the wisdom to work it, you'll never see fruit.

Vision alone is not enough. God expects you to **do something** with what He's shown you, and not just any doing; He expects **wise work**. There's a difference between activity and progress. Between being busy and being fruitful. Kingdom stewardship requires both—**wisdom to know what to do and the discipline to do it well.**

"Through wisdom a house is built, and by understanding it is established; by knowledge the rooms are filled..." — Proverbs 24:3–4

Notice the pattern: Wisdom builds. Understanding establishes. Knowledge fills.

God doesn't just hand you a finished house. He gives you **raw materials** and **spiritual intelligence, the divine insight and understanding, to build it.**

This chapter is about becoming a wise builder who turns vision into action and revelation into results.

SECTION 1. Wisdom Builds What Desire Alone Cannot

Desire is powerful. Passion is energizing. But **wisdom builds.**

"Through wisdom a house is built..." — Proverbs 24:3

This Scripture is true for literal houses, businesses, ministries, marriages, and personal growth. Wisdom is what turns vision into form. Passion may ignite movement, but **only wisdom sustains it.**

Many people fail in life, not because of a lack of vision but because of a lack of wise strategy. They love God. They pray fervently. However, their lives are disorganized, their finances are undisciplined, and their leadership is reactive rather than proactive.

Desire without wisdom is ineffective and dangerous. It can lead to missteps, wasted efforts, and even harm.

- You can desire a strong marriage, but without communication skills, it will collapse.
- You can want a successful business, but without financial literacy, you'll go broke.
- You can crave revival, but without order and discipleship, you'll only create chaos.

The danger of desire being alone is why Solomon asked for wisdom, not wealth, not status, not power. He knew wisdom was the well that produced everything else.

Every vision you carry requires a corresponding strategy from the Kingdom to bring it to life. It's wisdom that provides the roadmap, the 'how' behind the 'what;' it's a practical tool for achieving your goals.

SECTION 2. James 1 – Ask God for Wisdom

"If any of you lacks wisdom, let him ask of God, who gives generously to all without reproach..." — James 1:5

God never intended for you to figure life out on your own. He expects you to request wisdom, and He promises to **give it freely** to those who ask in faith. That means:
- You don't need to fake your way through a calling.
- You don't need to copy someone else's method.
- You don't need to guess your way into stewardship.

When we talk about 'asking,' it's not just about saying the words. It's about opening your heart and mind to receive God's guidance. **You can ask, and God will answer.**

Asking for wisdom should be part of your daily life:
- *"Lord, how do I handle this meeting today?"*
- *"God, what's the right tone for this conversation?"*
- *"Father, how should I price this product?"*
- *"Holy Spirit, what system should I set up in this ministry?"*

Wisdom is spiritual, but it shows up practically. When you ask, you receive **not just insight but instruction.**

The wisest people in scripture weren't the ones with the most experience. They were the ones who **kept asking.**

SECTION 3. The Diligence Factor

"The soul of the sluggard craves and gets nothing, while the soul of the diligent is richly supplied." — Proverbs 13:4

In the Kingdom, **diligence is faith in motion.** It's the muscle of stewardship. You can't pray your way around work, and you can't fast your way past discipline.

Diligence means:
- Showing up even when you don't feel it.

- Doing the work when no one sees it.
- Managing what you have, while trusting God for what's next.

Many believers wait for "divine acceleration" when what they need is consistent obedience. **God blesses faithfulness before He blesses fruitfulness.** The diligent steward will always outlast the distracted one.

"Whoever is slothful will not roast his game, but the diligent man will get precious wealth." — Proverbs 12:27

Some people are skilled hunters; they receive prophetic words, ideas, and even answered prayers, but lack follow-through. **Remember, it's not just about catching the** game; **it's about roasting it. It's about turning** what **you've** seen into something that feeds **you** and others.

Wisdom works, and wise people finish what they start.

SECTION 4. Ecclesiastes 10—Sharpen the Axe

"If the ax is dull and one does not sharpen the edge, then he must exert more strength; but wisdom brings success." — Ecclesiastes 10:10

Instead of swinging harder, consider the power of sharpening smarter.

Some people find themselves exhausted, not because the work is too big, but because their tools are too dull. They're grinding through life with blunted habits, broken systems, and outdated thinking. Imagine the relief that comes from efficient work, from sharpening your tools and lightening your load.

Wisdom sharpens you.
- It reveals the right timing.
- It upgrades your tools.
- It multiplies your effort with less wear and tear.

Stewardship doesn't always mean more effort. Sometimes, it means better effort.

Ask yourself:
- What in your life needs sharpening?
- What system do you need to revisit?
- What pattern is wasting time or energy?

Don't glorify grind when God has offered you guidance.

SECTION 5. Work as Worship

"Whatever you do, work at it with all your heart, as working for the Lord..." — Colossians 3:23

In the Kingdom, work is not just a means to an end; **it's a ministry.** When you work with wisdom and integrity, you're worshiping.

Your work becomes sacred when:
- You surrender your heart
- Your motives are pure
- Your excellence reflects God's glory

God doesn't just anoint preachers. He anoints plumbers, programmers, baristas, builders, educators, and entrepreneurs. The difference isn't the role—it's the posture.

Work becomes holy when it flows from revelation. You're not just doing tasks; you're executing vision.

That means how you send emails, lead meetings, clean your house, and build your product—all of it matters. When wisdom informs your endeavor, and your work becomes worship, you become unstoppable.

SECTION 6. Practical Tools to Steward Work and Wisdom

1. **Weekly Wisdom Retreat**
   Set aside 30 minutes each week to ask: "Lord, what's the wisest use of my time this week?" Journal the answer.

2. **The 'Sharpen List'**
   Make a list of tools, habits, and systems that feel dull or draining. Pray through which to upgrade, cut, or restructure.

3. **Skill Stewardship**
   What skill has God given you that needs sharpening? Read a book. Take a course. Practice. Don't bury your talent—multiply it.

4. **Workflow Audit**
   List everything you're doing. Then ask: "Is this wise, or just busy?" Wisdom is not about doing more; it's about doing what matters.

SECTION 7. **Reflection Questions**

1. What area of my life am I trying to build without wisdom?
2. Where have I confused activity with effectiveness?
3. What dull area of my life needs sharpening?
4. How can I make my work more like worship this week?

SECTION 8. **Prayer Declaration**

Father, I thank You for wisdom. I renounce foolish striving and ask for Your insight. Help me to build wisely, to work diligently, and to worship You through my daily labor. Let my hands reflect Your excellence. Let Your word shape my decisions. I declare that wisdom is guiding me, diligence is strengthening me, and fruitfulness is following me. In Jesus' name, amen.

Chapter 4.2

Understanding Seasons

Scripture Focus:
Ecclesiastes 3:1, Galatians 6:9, 1 Chronicles 12:32

Ecclesiastes 3:1 (KJV) *1 To every thing there is a season, and a time to every purpose under the heaven:*

Galatians 6:9 (KJV) *9 And let us not be weary in well doing: for in due season we shall reap, if we faint not.*

1 Chronicles 12:32 (KJV) *32 And of the children of Issachar, which were men that had understanding of the times, to know what Israel ought to do; the heads of them were two hundred; and all their brethren were at their commandment.*

INTRODUCTION. Why Seasons Matter

One of the most overlooked aspects of stewardship is **timing**. You can do the right thing at the wrong time and still miss God's will. That's why wisdom must be paired with discernment, because **fruitfulness is seasonal.**

> *"To everything there is a season, a time for every purpose under heaven." — Ecclesiastes 3:1*

God doesn't just assign vision; He ordains seasons. Each one carries unique instructions. What works in one season may not be effective in the next. When you understand the season you're in, you'll know:
- When to sow
- When to reap
- When to rest
- When to fight

- When to wait
- When to speak

Discerning seasons helps you say no to seemingly good things so you can say yes to the **things of God.**

This chapter will show you how to recognize your season, respond in faith, and remain fruitful, **regardless of the time.**

SECTION 1. The Sons of Issachar—Discerning the Times

"...the sons of Issachar who had understanding of the times, to know what Israel ought to do..." — 1 Chronicles 12:32

The sons of Issachar were not renowned for their physical strength or skill. Their actual distinction lay in their **discernment**. They had a profound understanding of the times, and because of that, they knew what to do.

What distinguishes leaders who merely survive from those who **truly steward well** is not just their grasp of the truth but their understanding of **timing.**

In leadership, business, and ministry, you will face crossroads that require more than experience. They require spiritual insight:

- *Is it time to expand or scale back?*
- *Should I push forward or pause?*
- *Is this a harvest season or a pruning season?*

Issachar-level wisdom is the kind that listens before leaping. It perceives before working. It recognizes that **seasonal ignorance can lead to spiritual exhaustion.**

A steward must not only ask: *What has God said?* But also: *What is God saying* now?

SECTION 2. Ecclesiastes—A Time for Everything

"There is a time to plant and a time to uproot..." — Ecclesiastes 3:2

Ecclesiastes Chapter 3 outlines 28 paired seasons—times to laugh, weep, embrace, refrain, gain, lose, and so on. Each season carries a distinct purpose, and that's what many people miss.

There's nothing wrong with the season you're in; it's what you do with it that matters.
- If it's a planting season, don't demand a harvest.
- If it's a pruning season, don't fear the cuts.
- If it's a waiting season, don't confuse silence with absence.

You wouldn't yell at a tree in winter for not bearing fruit, knowing that it's simply not the right season for it. So why do we yell at our lives in winter seasons?

Stewardship means cooperating with the climate God has you in because every season has a divine assignment.

SECTION 3. The Danger of Misreading Your Season

One of the greatest threats to Kingdom productivity is **misinterpreting the season you're in.**

Some signs you've misread your season:
- You're frustrated by what God never promised for now
- You're comparing your pace to someone in a harvest while you're still in preparation
- You're overworking when you should be resting
- You're retreating when you should be building

Moses struck the rock in anger because he misread his moment. Saul sacrificed without Samuel because he misread the urgency. Both were anointed, but both **lost momentum because they moved out of sync with God.**

Misreading seasons leads to mismanagement.

When you force a harvest in a planting season, you'll feel disappointed. When you try to rest in a war season, you'll feel overwhelmed. You don't need to fear the season; you need to **discern it.**

SECTION 4. Galatians 6—Do Not Grow Weary

"Let us not become weary in doing good, for at the proper time we will reap a harvest if we do not give up." — Galatians 6:9

This verse assures us that the **harvest is seasonal,** and a delayed reward should never be mistaken for denial. The harvest is inevitable.

But there's a catch: **weariness is real,** and weariness tempts stewards to quit too soon. This weariness can manifest in various forms, from physical exhaustion to emotional burnout. Recognize the signs and persevere.

When you don't see results, when nothing seems to move, when the people you're helping don't seem to care, that's when **discouragement distorts perspective.**

You start thinking:
- "Maybe I missed God."
- "Maybe I'm not good at this."
- "Maybe I should try something else."

But Paul says: *keep going.* The harvest is guaranteed **if** you don't give up. That "if" is where stewardship lives.

God won't do the work for you. But He will sustain you through the wait if you remain faithful in the field.

SECTION 5. How to Steward a New Season

When God shifts your season, everything doesn't always feel different. Sometimes, it starts with a whisper, a restlessness, a redirection, a fresh grace for a new rhythm.

Wise stewards don't just enter a new season; they prepare for it. Here's how to steward a season well:

1. **Recognize It**
   Ask the Holy Spirit, *"What time is it in my life?"* Sometimes, the season won't be evident until you ask.

2. **Release the Old**
   New seasons require new mindsets. You cannot take winter habits into a spring assignment. Let go of what no longer serves your calling.

3. **Recommit to the Process**
   Every season brings a process, including growth and change. Don't rush it. Don't resent it. Steward it with trust and diligence.
4. **Realign Your Actions**
   Adjust your daily life to match your divine season. That includes schedule, spending, priorities, and relationships. This act of realignment will help you feel focused and more prepared throughout your journey.

Stewardship without seasonal awareness leads to frustration. But when you honor what God is doing *now*, you'll carry peace even when the path isn't clear.

SECTION 6. Tools for Seasonal Discernment

1. **Monthly Quiet Time Retreat**
   Once a month, take a few hours to ask: "Lord, what season am I in?" Journal His impressions and any scriptures He highlights.
2. **The 90-Day Check-In**
   Every quarter, evaluate: What fruit is showing? Where's the grace flowing? What's draining me that used to energize me?
3. **Circle of Counsel**
   Consult with a spiritual mentor who understands your spiritual journey. Ask them what they discern about your timing. God often confirms seasons through wise voices.
4. **Scripture Season Tracker**
   As you read the Word, ask: What season was this person in? (e.g., David in the cave, Joseph in prison, Paul in mission). Learn how they stewarded it and apply it.

SECTION 7. Reflection Questions

1. What season am I in right now—planting, pruning, waiting, reaping, resting, rebuilding?
2. Am I resisting the season or cooperating with it?
3. What do I need to release in order to embrace this season fully?
4. Who do I need to invite to help me discern the timing of my next step?

SECTION 8. **Prayer Declaration**

Father, I thank You for seasons. You are the God of rhythm, timing, and purpose. Help me discern the time I'm in. I reject frustration and embrace alignment. I declare that I am not behind, I am not late, and I am not forgotten. I will reap in due season. I will not grow weary. I trust Your process. In Jesus' name, amen.

Chapter 4.3

Grace for the Grind

Scripture Focus:
1 Corinthians 15:10, Matthew 11:28–30,
2 Corinthians 12:9

1 Corinthians 15:10 (KJV) *10 But by the grace of God I am what I am: and his grace which was bestowed upon me was not in vain; but I laboured more abundantly than they all: yet not I, but the grace of God which was with me.*

Matthew 11:28-30 (KJV) *28 Come unto me, all ye that labour and are heavy laden, and I will give you rest. 29 Take my yoke upon you, and learn of me; for I am meek and lowly in heart: and ye shall find rest unto your souls. 30 For my yoke is easy, and my burden is light.*

2 Corinthians 12:9 (KJV) *9 And he said unto me, My grace is sufficient for thee: for my strength is made perfect in weakness. Most gladly therefore will I rather glory in my infirmities, that the power of Christ may rest upon me.*

INTRODUCTION. When Grit Meets Grace

There's a word our culture celebrates: **grind**. Push harder. Sleep less. Hustle more. Build your dream. Never stop.

While there is much value in hard work, there's also a danger in turning hustle into **idolatry**. In the Kingdom, **grace powers productivity**, not panic.

> *"But by the grace of God I am what I am, and His grace toward me was not in vain; I worked harder than all of them—yet not I, but the grace of God that was with me."* — 1 Corinthians 15:10

Paul understood what many of us forget: it wasn't just his effort; it was **grace in his work.** This kind of grace means that even when we work hard, we do so with a sense of God's favor and assistance, which can alleviate the stress and pressure often associated with hard work.

God doesn't call you to burnout He calls you to **grace-powered stewardship,** which means managing your time, energy, and resources in a way that is sustainable and honors God. For example, it could mean setting boundaries in your work, taking regular breaks, and prioritizing self-care.

This chapter will help you:
- Work without being worn out
- Stay diligent without becoming drained
- Walk in a rhythm of rest, excellence, and joy

Because **grace doesn't eliminate the grind; it transforms it.**

SECTION 1. Paul—Working Hard by Grace

"...I worked harder than all of them—yet not I, but the grace of God that was with me." — 1 Corinthians 15:10

Paul was no stranger to labor. He planted churches, wrote letters, trained leaders, and endured beatings, imprisonments, and shipwrecks. He was **productive but not panicked.** His strength didn't come from caffeine or the energy of the crowds; it came from **grace.**

He didn't say, "I did it all." He said, "God's grace did it through me."

There's a unique type of Kingdom work that may appear as striving, but it's surrender. It's about working *alongside* God, not just *for* Him. This shift in perspective should transform the way we approach our tasks.

Paul's grind was marked by:
- Focus without frenzy
- Movement without burnout
- Passion without pressure

That's the power of grace: **it multiplies your effort without draining your soul.**

If your grind is making you bitter, burned out, or broken, it's not powered by grace. It may be time to pause and ask: *"God, did You assign this?"* Because what God assigns, He also **empowers you to complete it.**

SECTION 2. Matthew 11—The Easy Yoke

> *"Come to Me, all you who are weary and burdened, and I will give you rest... Take My yoke upon you and learn from Me... For My yoke is easy and My burden is light."* — Matthew 11:28–30

Jesus didn't promise a life free from labor. He promised a **different kind of burden.** A yoke is a work tool; it connects two oxen to plow together.

When Jesus invites us to take His yoke, He's saying:
"Let Me do the heavy lifting. Learn how I work. Let Me set the pace."

Some of us are growing weary because we're dragging a yoke **He never asked us to carry.** We may have said yes out of guilt or kept going because we felt needed. We may be doing everything *except* what He's asked of us.

Grace is found **inside His assignment.** Outside of it, you'll feel pressure. Inside it, you'll feel power. This power is not our own, but it comes from aligning with Jesus' purpose for us.

The "grind" becomes grace-filled when it's yoked to Jesus' rhythm. This rhythm brings balance and harmony to our lives, relieving us from the unnecessary burdens we often carry.

SECTION 3. How Grace Fuels True Productivity

Grace is not the absence of work. It's the **presence of God's empowering strength** in your work.

> *"My grace is sufficient for you, for My power is made perfect in weakness..."* — 2 Corinthians 12:9

Paul wasn't celebrating exhaustion; he was celebrating **dependence.** He recognized that what made him effective wasn't his résumé; it was the **divine enablement,** such as sudden bursts of inspiration, unexpected solutions to problems, or a sense of peace amid chaos, that met him in his weakness.

Here's what grace-powered productivity looks like:
- You produce without panic
- You create with clarity
- You lead with joy, not resentment
- You meet deadlines without feeling defeated
- You say *no* when needed because you trust God's provision

Grace empowers you to stop trying to prove yourself and **partner with God.**

When grace is on you:
- Five hours of work produces what ten used to
- One conversation accomplishes what weeks of striving couldn't
- One "yes" from God outweighs dozens of human opportunities

Grace multiplies what surrender gives it.

SECTION 4. Warning Signs of Grinding Without Grace

Sometimes, the red flags are emotional. Sometimes, they're physical. But when you're grinding outside of grace, it will show.

Here are signs you're working from the wrong source:
- **Chronic exhaustion:** You're constantly tired, even after rest.
- **Emotional volatility:** Small things trigger significant reactions. You're snappy, cynical, or numb.
- **Performance pressure:** You feel like you can't stop, can't fail, and can't say no.
- **Neglect of spiritual rhythms:** You skip prayer, Word time, or worship because "you're too busy."
- **Bitterness toward the people you serve:** You love the mission, but you secretly resent the ones you're serving.

Reminder: Grace never leads you into places where intimacy with God becomes impossible.

SECTION 5. Practical Rhythms of Grace

Grace doesn't make you lazy; it makes you strategic. It leads to *rhythms*, not *ruts*. Here are five ways to build a grace-filled structure into your life:

1. **Sabbath Non-Negotiables**
   Pick a day each week when you don't work. No emails. No meetings. No, "just one more thing." Let your soul breathe.
2. **Morning Alignment**
   Before you open your calendar, open the Word. Ask, "God, what's **mine** to carry today?" Let Him set your priorities.
3. **Margin Breaks**
   Schedule breathing room between major tasks. Give your brain permission to rest, not just your body.
4. **Assignment Filters**
   Before saying yes, ask: *"Is this in my grace zone, or am I driven by guilt or fear?"* Never trade obedience for obligation.
5. **Grace Check Journaling**
   Once a week, reflect:
   - What drained me?
   - What energized me?
   - Did I operate in striving or in a Spirit-led flow?

Stewarding grace takes intentionality, but it pays off in joy, longevity, and clarity.

SECTION 6. Reflection Questions

1. Where in my life am I operating in grind rather than grace?
2. What signs of burnout or striving have I been ignoring?
3. What rhythms do I need to add or restore to walk in grace?
4. What assignment do I need to release so I can rest?

SECTION 7. Prayer Declaration

Father, thank You for Your empowering grace. I lay down the burden of proving, striving, and performing. I receive Your rhythm. Teach me to work with You, not just for You. Fill me with wisdom, energy, and holy rest. I declare that I am not driven; I am led. I am not grinding; I am graced. In Jesus' name, amen.

Chapter 4.4

The Blessing of Work

Scripture Focus:
Genesis 2:15, Colossians 3:23–24, Proverbs 14:23, Ecclesiastes 5:18–19

Genesis 2:15 (KJV) *15 And the LORD God took the man, and put him into the garden of Eden to dress it and to keep it.*

Colossians 3:23-24 (KJV) *23 And whatsoever ye do, do it heartily, as to the Lord, and not unto men; 24 Knowing that of the Lord ye shall receive the reward of the inheritance: for ye serve the Lord Christ.*

Proverbs 14:23 (KJV) *23 In all labour there is profit: but the talk of the lips tendeth only to penury.*

Ecclesiastes 5:18-19 (KJV) *18 Behold that which I have seen: it is good and comely for one to eat and to drink, and to enjoy the good of all his labour that he taketh under the sun all the days of his life, which God giveth him: for it is his portion. 19 Every man also to whom God hath given riches and wealth, and hath given him power to eat thereof, and to take his portion, and to rejoice in his labour; this is the gift of God.*

INTRODUCTION. Work is Not a Curse

In the Kingdom, **work is not punishment; it's purpose.**

Many people believe that labor entered the world after sin. But the Bible says:

> *"The Lord God took the man and put him in the Garden of Eden to work it and take care of it."* — Genesis 2:15

That was before the fall, which means **work was part of God's perfect plan.**

Work was not the result of the curse. *Toil* was. *Frustration* was. *Futility* was.

But work itself? **Work is holy.**

The moment God gave Adam breath, He gave him responsibility. Why? Because God created Man not just to receive but to **be fruitful,** to **multiply,** to **replenish,** to **subdue,** and to **have dominion** (Gen 1:28).

This chapter will help you:
- Reframe your mindset about labor
- Recover joy in your assignments
- Recognize the spiritual significance of your everyday responsibilities

Because when you see your work as worship, even the mundane becomes meaningful.

SECTION 1. Genesis—Work Was the Original Assignment

"The Lord God took the man and put him in the garden of Eden to work it and keep it." — Genesis 2:15

The first gift God gave man—before marriage, before ministry—was a **job.**

He gave Adam a garden, not to sit and admire, but to **steward:**
- Cultivate it
- Guard it
- Multiply it
- Protect its boundaries

That means work is not the result of brokenness; it's part of your **blueprint.**

In fact, the Hebrew word for "work" in this verse is *abad*, which also means **worship** or **service.** So, when you work, you're not just earning a paycheck; you're honoring God's original purpose for your life.

Your job may not feel "spiritual," but in the eyes of the Kingdom, **faithful stewardship of your assignment is worship.**

Remember, God doesn't just see a divide between sacred and secular—He sees **obedience and commitment** in every task, guiding you in a way that makes **faithfulness not optional.**

When you do what He's called you to do, whether it's parenting, building, managing, or serving, **you are walking in the Eden mandate.**

SECTION 2. Colossians—Work as Unto the Lord

"Whatever you do, work at it with all your heart, as working for the Lord, not for men." — Colossians 3:23

Paul doesn't say, *"If it's ministry, work hard."* He says, *"Whatever you do."*

In God's economy:
- Teaching a child and managing a business are both sacred
- Cleaning a house and leading a revival can both carry eternal value
- Excellence is worship, regardless of the audience

You don't need a stage to glorify God. You need a spirit of excellence.

When you realize God is your ultimate Boss, your perspective shifts:
- You stop performing for people
- You start preparing with a purpose
- You stop clocking in with dread
- You start showing up with joy

Remember, **you're not just working; you're worshipping.** Every task, no matter how small or seemingly insignificant, is an opportunity to glorify God through your spirit of excellence.

SECTION 3. Proverbs—Diligence Produces Results

"All hard work brings a profit, but mere talk leads only to poverty."
— Proverbs 14:23

Solomon didn't just promote hard work; he drew a clear contrast:
- **Hard work brings results**
- **Empty talk brings lack**

Hard work vs. lack isn't just about finances; **it's about fruitfulness in every area of life.**

Diligence isn't working harder than others; it's working with focus, consistency, and intentionality. It's showing up when it's not glamorous. It's finishing what you start. It's refusing to let distractions derail your discipline.

In the Kingdom, effort matters. Not to earn salvation but to express **stewardship.**

Proverbs also says:

"The hand of the diligent will rule..." — Proverbs 12:24

Diligence brings promotion. It unlocks favor. It builds credibility and influence.

You can pray for a breakthrough, but diligence is often the key that unlocks it.

SECTION 4. **Ecclesiastes—Work Is a Gift**

"It is good and proper for a man to eat and drink, and to enjoy the good of all his labor... it is the gift of God." — Ecclesiastes 5:18–19

Sometimes, we only view work as an obligation. But Solomon called it a **gift.**

God wired you to build, produce, create, solve, and contribute. When you work on your assignment, you experience fulfillment, not just fatigue.

For instance, if you're a teacher, you can find joy and purpose in your work by seeing the growth and development of your students. That's why burnout often doesn't come from doing too much; it comes from doing things that **lack joy and purpose.**

When you align your work with God's purpose, you can experience:
- Deep satisfaction
- A sense of eternal value
- Joy in the journey

Work becomes a gift **when it's received with gratitude and done with excellence.**

SECTION 5. **Recovering Joy in Your Assignment**

Somewhere along the way, many of us lost our joy in what we once prayed for.

We asked God for the job, the business, the opportunity, then slowly began resenting the weight of responsibility. But it's crucial to remember **Who we're working for and why He called us to it.**

To recover joy in your assignment, ask yourself:

1. **Who am I ultimately serving?**
   If the answer is the Lord, then the smallest task carries eternal significance, bringing a deep sense of fulfillment and joy.
2. **What lives are being touched through this work?**
   Think beyond the task. Who benefits from your consistency?
3. **How can I realign this role with my purpose?**
   Even in a difficult season, God may be using this work to refine you for something greater.

Joy comes when you stop enduring your job, which implies a sense of suffering or tolerating, and start engaging it as a form of **obedience and worship.** Engaging your job means actively participating in it, finding meaning in it, and doing it with a sense of purpose.

"The joy of the Lord is your strength." — Nehemiah 8:10 And His joy shows up in the middle of your assignment, not just at the end of it.

SECTION 6. **Reflection Questions**

1. Have I seen work as a burden instead of a blessing?
2. Where have I been showing up with my body but not with my heart?
3. How can I realign my daily responsibilities with worship?
4. What would change if I saw my work as a sacred assignment?

SECTION 7. **Prayer Declaration**

Father, thank You for the gift of work. Forgive me for every time I've complained, slacked, or resented my assignments. I choose to see work as worship. I declare that my hands are blessed, my mind is focused, and my labor is not in vain. I show up with excellence, and I do it for Your glory. In Jesus' name, amen.

Chapter 4.5

Wisdom for Work and Wealth

Scripture Focus:
Proverbs 3:13–16, James 1:5, Ecclesiastes 10:10, Proverbs 24:3–4

Proverbs 3:13-16 (KJV) *13 Happy is the man that findeth wisdom, and the man that getteth understanding. 14 For the merchandise of it is better than the merchandise of silver, and the gain thereof than fine gold. 15 She is more precious than rubies: and all the things thou canst desire are not to be compared unto her. 16 Length of days is in her right hand; and in her left hand riches and honour.*

James 1:5 (KJV) *5 If any of you lack wisdom, let him ask of God, that giveth to all men liberally, and upbraideth not; and it shall be given him.*

Ecclesiastes 10:10 (KJV) *10 If the iron be blunt, and he do not whet the edge, then must he put to more strength: but wisdom is profitable to direct.*

Proverbs 24:3-4 (KJV) *3 Through wisdom is an house builded; and by understanding it is established: 4 And by knowledge shall the chambers be filled with all precious and pleasant riches.*

INTRODUCTION. It Takes More Than Effort

Hard work is essential, but **it is not enough by itself.**

You can sweat and struggle and still stay stuck. Why? Because in the Kingdom, fruitfulness requires **wisdom.**

"Wisdom is more precious than rubies, and nothing you desire can compare with her." — Proverbs 3:15

Many people are burning out, not because they lack effort but because they lack a clear **strategy.** They don't need more hours in the day. **They need the empowerment of wisdom to bring more clarity to their decisions.**

Wisdom isn't just about being smart; **it's about knowing what to do. When to do it. How to do it, and with whom to do it.**

And it all comes **from God, our Source** of wisdom.

This chapter will help you:
- Recognize the difference between effort and effectiveness
- Ask God for wisdom in practical areas
- Build your life, work, and wealth on Kingdom strategy, not just human strength

Because wisdom doesn't just build success; it sustains it.

SECTION 1. **Proverbs—Wisdom Brings Wealth and Honor**

"Blessed are those who find wisdom... She is more profitable than silver and yields better returns than gold." — Proverbs 3:13–14

Solomon, the wealthiest man of his time, didn't ask God for money. He asked for **wisdom.** And as a result, God gave him everything else.

Why? Because:
- Wisdom knows where to invest
- Wisdom knows how to discern timing
- Wisdom knows how to avoid traps
- Wisdom knows who to trust

"By wisdom a house is built, and through understanding it is established; through knowledge its rooms are filled with rare and beautiful treasures." — Proverbs 24:3–4

Effort without wisdom leads to **exhaustion.** But when you walk in wisdom, you experience **overflow,** not just financially but relationally, spiritually, and generationally.

Wisdom is not just good advice; it's **divine insight** that makes work productive and ensures that wealth is sustainable.

SECTION 2. James—Ask God for Wisdom

"If any of you lacks wisdom, you should ask God, who gives generously to all without finding fault…" — James 1:5

Sometimes we forget that **wisdom is a promise, not a privilege.** God doesn't give wisdom based on seniority; He gives it based on **sincerity.**

If you ask in faith, He will answer with clarity.

Here's the catch: when wisdom comes, it may not sound like what you would expect. It might tell you:
- To slow down
- To say no
- To wait
- To delegate
- To stop spending
- To invest where others won't

Wisdom rarely shouts. It whispers to the humble. So, if you're overwhelmed, don't ask for help first; **ask for wisdom.** Help will only fix the surface. Wisdom will fix the system.

SECTION 3. Ecclesiastes—Sharpen the Axe

"If the ax is dull and its edge unsharpened, more strength is needed, but skill will bring success." — Ecclesiastes 10:10

You don't need a bigger axe—you need a sharper one. In other words, **skill is more potent than mere effort.**

The wisdom in skill is the difference between hustle and mastery:
- Hustle says, "Do more."
- Wisdom says, "Do it better."
- Hustle burns out.
- Wisdom builds up.

Ask yourself:
- What tools am I using that need sharpening?

- What systems have I outgrown?
- Where am I applying pressure when I should be seeking perspective?

The sharpest leaders aren't always the busiest; they're the ones who know when to **step back, sharpen, and strike at the right angle.**

SECTION 4. How Wisdom Builds Wealth

The Kingdom measures wealth not by money alone but by **what lasts.** Wisdom builds wealth that outlives you:
- Financial wealth
- Relational wealth
- Spiritual wealth
- Legacy wealth

"The wise store up choice food and olive oil, but fools gulp theirs down." — Proverbs 21:20

Wisdom doesn't just earn; it preserves. It knows how to:
- Budget wisely
- Multiply resources
- Create systems
- Avoid waste
- Sow with vision
- Grow with integrity

Wealth built through hard work can be lost in an instant. However, wealth built on wisdom will survive storms and volatile markets, lasting for generations.

That's why Kingdom stewards choose to pursue wisdom before they pursue opportunity.

SECTION 5. Practical Wisdom Disciplines

Wisdom grows with practice. Here are five ways to develop it daily:

1. **Begin Every Day with a Wisdom Prayer**
   "Lord, give me clarity, timing, and discernment for every decision today."

2. **Read a Chapter of Proverbs Daily**
   There are 31 chapters, one for each day. The more you read, the more your instincts align with the truth.
3. **Ask More Questions Than You Answer**
   Wise people are learners. Seek counsel. Interview mentors. Study patterns.
4. **Learn from Your Mistakes**
   When things go wrong, don't just feel frustrated; ask, "What is wisdom teaching me here?"
5. **Surround Yourself with Wise People**

   "Walk with the wise and become wise..." — Proverbs 13:20

   Your circle is your curriculum.

SECTION 6. Reflection Questions

1. Where have I been relying on effort more than wisdom?
2. What area of my life or work needs sharpening right now?
3. What daily habits can I form to grow in wisdom?
4. Whom should I seek counsel or mentorship from?

SECTION 7. Prayer Declaration

Father, I thank You for being the source of all wisdom. I lay down pride, confusion, and exhaustion. I ask for clarity in my calling, skill in my work, and discernment in my decisions. I declare that I operate with divine strategy and steward every opportunity with insight. I don't just work hard—I work wisely. In Jesus' name, amen.

Chapter 4.6

Multiplying with Wisdom

Scripture Focus:
Matthew 25:14–30, Proverbs 21:5, Luke 16:10–12

Matthew 25:14-30 (KJV) *14 For the kingdom of heaven is as a man travelling into a far country, who called his own servants, and delivered unto them his goods. 15 And unto one he gave five talents, to another two, and to another one; to every man according to his several ability; and straightway took his journey. 16 Then he that had received the five talents went and traded with the same, and made them other five talents. 17 And likewise he that had received two, he also gained other two. 18 But he that had received one went and digged in the earth, and hid his lord's money. 19 After a long time the lord of those servants cometh, and reckoneth with them. 20 And so he that had received five talents came and brought other five talents, saying, Lord, thou deliveredst unto me five talents: behold, I have gained beside them five talents more. 21 His lord said unto him, Well done, thou good and faithful servant: thou hast been faithful over a few things, I will make thee ruler over many things: enter thou into the joy of thy lord. 22 He also that had received two talents came and said, Lord, thou deliveredst unto me two talents: behold, I have gained two other talents beside them. 23 His lord said unto him, Well done, good and faithful servant; thou hast been faithful over a few things, I will make thee ruler over many things: enter thou into the joy of thy lord. 24 Then he which had received the one talent came and said, Lord, I knew thee that thou art an hard man, reaping where thou hast not sown, and gathering where thou hast not strawed: 25 And I was afraid, and went and hid thy talent in the earth: lo, there thou hast that is thine. 26 His lord* *answered and said unto him, Thou wicked and slothful servant, thou knewest that I reap where I sowed not, and gather where I have not strawed: 27 Thou oughtest therefore to have put my money to the exchangers, and then at my coming I should have received mine own with usury. 28 Take therefore the talent from him, and give it unto him which hath ten talents. 29 For unto every one that hath shall be given, and he shall have abundance: but from him that hath not shall be taken away even that which he hath. 30 And cast ye the unprofitable servant into outer darkness: there shall be weeping and gnashing of teeth.*

Proverbs 21:5 (KJV) *5 The thoughts of the diligent tend only to plenteousness; but of every one that is hasty only to want.*

Luke 16:10-12 (KJV) *10. He that is faithful in that which is least is faithful also in much: and he that is unjust in the least is unjust also in much. 11. If therefore ye have not been faithful in the unrighteous mammon, who will commit to your trust the true riches? 12. And if ye have not been faithful in that which is another man's, who shall give you that which is your own?*

INTRODUCTION. God Doesn't Just Bless Effort, He Rewards Multiplication

One of the most overlooked truths in the Bible is this: **God rewards growth.** God is not just a God of maintenance; He's a God of **multiplication.** In every area of stewardship—money, time, talent, and resources—He expects **increase.**

> *"To one he gave five talents... to another two... to another one... each according to his several ability."* — Matthew 25:15

In the parable of the Talents (Matthew 25), each servant was given something. They were not judged by how much they had but **by what they did with what they had.** Only those who multiplied what they were given were rewarded.

Many believe that faithfulness means **holding on, protecting, or maintaining** what's been entrusted. But in the Kingdom, faithfulness means **multiplying. God doesn't expect you to multiply what you weren't given, but He does expect fruit from what you have.**

God is not a manager; He's a multiplier, and **He's looking for stewards who think the same.**

This truth challenges the religious mindset that says, *"If I just don't lose it, I've done well."* But Jesus called the one-talent servant, who returned precisely what he was given, **wicked and lazy.**

Why? Because he feared loss more than he honored the Lord with his assignment.

Many believers pray for increase, yet they are stewards who think like maintainers. But in the Kingdom, **faithfulness isn't just about holding ground—it's about taking ground, about being proactive and assertive in your faithfulness.**

This chapter is about reclaiming your biblical authority to **multiply what God has given you,** whether it's a skill, a resource, a ministry, a relationship, or an opportunity. And it's about doing it with **wisdom, not just hard work.**

This chapter will help you:
- Understand the biblical mandate for multiplication
- Recognize how wisdom plays a role in your increase
- Multiply what God has put in your hands with intentionality and strategy

We'll explore how godly multiplication works, why many avoid it, and how you can embrace your calling as a **faithful multiplier** in every season. Because **you are called to multiply, not just manage.**

SECTION 1. The Parable of the Talents— Multiplication Is the Mandate

"To one he gave five talents, to another two, and to another one, to each according to his ability..." — Matthew 25:15

In this well-known parable, Jesus clarified one thing: **God settles accounts.** He returns to see what you've done with what He entrusted. **Everyone is entrusted with something.**

No one is talentless in the Kingdom. What differs is the **measure**, not the **mandate**.

The Master gives to each *"according to his ability,"* which reveals an important truth:

- God doesn't compare what He has given you to what He gave someone else
- He holds you accountable for what He entrusted to **you**

What Did They Do?

- The servant with five talents doubled it.
- The one with two did the same.
- But the one with one talent buried it and was rebuked.

Two multiplied. One played it safe.

The issue wasn't the amount; it was the **mindset**.

The first two operated with courage and creativity. The third operated in fear and excuse:

"I knew you were a hard man..." (v. 24)

And here's the surprise: The Master gave **the same praise** to the one who returned ten and the one who returned four: *"Well done, good and faithful servant."*

God measures faithfulness **by growth, not amount.**

God doesn't reward potential; He rewards **faithful multiplication.** Not everyone will receive the same gifts and talents, nor will they be called to the same vocation, but **God will hold everyone accountable for their stewardship.**

Multiplication isn't greed—it's **godliness.** It shows:

- Honor for the Giver
- Obedience to the assignment
- Readiness for promotion

The Master didn't say, *"Well thought out."* **He said,** *"Well done."*

The one who buried his talent gave a rehearsed speech:

- *"I knew you to be a hard man..."*
- *"I was afraid..."*
- *"So, I hid what you gave me..."*

This servant didn't squander it recklessly; he squandered it **passively.**

He missed the reward, not because he sinned outwardly, but because he feared inwardly.

In the Kingdom, **fear of failure can be as dangerous as open rebellion.**

This section shows us that stewardship isn't just about **safekeeping.** It's about **strategic growth**—a mindset of **multiplying with wisdom** rather than preserving in fear.

SECTION 2. Proverbs—Wise Plans Lead to Profit

"The plans of the diligent lead surely to abundance, but everyone who is hasty comes only to poverty." — Proverbs 21:5 (ESV)

This verse sharply contrasts two types of people: the **diligent planner** and the **hasty reactor.** One builds toward **abundance,** and the other falls into **lack,** not because of a lack of effort, but because of a lack of wisdom.

We live in a culture obsessed with speed, virality, and instant gratification. But Kingdom wealth, whether financial, relational, or spiritual, requires **strategy, structure, and sustainability.**

This verse gives us a multiplication blueprint:
- **Diligence** — Consistent, focused action
- **Planning** — Strategic execution over random effort
- **Patience** — Long-term thinking over short-term gratification

Wisdom doesn't just pray for multiplication; it **prepares** for it. **Let's break it down:**

1. **"The Plans"**
God doesn't bless confusion. He blesses clarity. **Planning is not unspiritual; it's essential.** Joseph had a plan for famine, Nehemiah had a plan for rebuilding, and Jesus had a plan for redemption. Planning is spiritual. **God Himself is a planner:**
   - He planned creation in six structured days (Genesis 1)
   - He planned redemption through Christ from the foundation of the world (1 Peter 1:20)
   - He planned the Tabernacle with detailed blueprints (Exodus 25–27)

A steward who desires multiplication must **embrace planning.** That includes:
- Business plans
- Budget forecasts
- Schedules
- Delegation systems
- Communication structures
- Succession and scaling strategies

Prayer and planning are not enemies—they are allies.

2. **"...of the Diligent"**
Not impulsive. Not wishful. Not random.
Diligence is sustained attention over time. It means you:
- Keep showing up
- Keep improving
- Keep evaluating and adjusting

Many people pray for profit but avoid the process. **Diligence is where breakthrough happens.**

3. **"...lead surely to abundance."**
The promise is **abundance,** not just survival.
When wisdom and work align, the outcome is **overflow.** That overflow becomes:
- Capacity for generosity
- Margin for creativity
- Resources for building
- Peace in the process

But here's the catch: **abundance doesn't arrive suddenly; it comes surely.**

God blesses the steward who thinks **ahead**, not just works hard.

Don't just chase results; design systems and build sustainability.

SECTION 3. Luke—Faithful in Little, Trusted with More

"One who is faithful in a very little is also faithful in much..." — Luke 16:10

This Scripture highlights the Kingdom principle of scale: **What you do with small reveals what you'll do with more. God watches how you handle small things to determine if you're ready for more.**
- If you cut corners with $100, you'll mismanage $10,000.
- If you slack with two followers, you'll mishandle two thousand.
- You won't steward a staff properly if you can't honor a small team.

Many want multiplication but skip the "little" phase. But in the Kingdom, **how you handle "little" sets the ceiling for your "much."**

What Does "Faithful in Little" Look Like?
- Finishing the task even when no one's watching
- Tracking small expenses with integrity
- Managing a small team with excellence
- Being grateful and responsible even when you feel overlooked
- Preparing today like tomorrow depends on it

God multiplies through trust. If you want God to entrust you with cities, you must first be faithful with **the one field He gave you.**

The fastest way to your next level is to overdeliver at your current one.

"Much" Doesn't Always Mean More Money

It can mean:
- Greater spiritual authority
- Increased leadership influence
- Expanded vision
- Doors of opportunity you couldn't manufacture

But these come **after** you prove consistency, not before.

SECTION 4. Multiply What You've Been Given

Multiplication begins with what you already have, not what you wish you had.

"What do you have in your hand?" — Exodus 4:2

When Moses doubted his calling, God didn't give him a new resource; He pointed to what was already in his hand.

This Scripture reveals the core principle of multiplication: **you don't need more—you need to see what you have differently.**

What's in Your Hand?

- A skill that solves problems
- A network of people you've underutilized
- A business that needs refining
- A small audience that needs consistent value
- A message that needs more structure and boldness

Multiplication begins with recognition. It's not about having more; it's about doing more with what you have.

If you despise what's in your hand, you'll never steward it to its full potential. Recognize the value in what you have. If you're always chasing what's in someone else's hand, you'll miss the miracle in yours.

Faith doesn't fantasize—it works with what's present and unlocks what's possible.

The servants in Matthew 25 started with what they received. The Master didn't give them more upfront; He gave them room to **multiply it.**

And how did they do it? Scripture doesn't give the process, but we can infer that it required:

- Initiative
- Strategy
- Risk
- Faith
- Diligence

Multiplication is always intentional. It doesn't happen accidentally.

Every great business, ministry, invention, and movement began with **a tiny yes.**

Wisdom doesn't wait—it works with what's available.

And as you do:

- Capacity grows
- Favor increases
- And God breathes on your obedience

So, what's in your hand? Identify it. Honor it. Multiply it.

SECTION 5. Scaling with Strategy

Multiplication without structure leads to collapse. That's why **scaling requires wisdom.**

Many people experience short bursts of growth, but without effective systems, this growth can become a burden. What was once a blessing turns into burnout.

Here's how to multiply with structure:

1. **Evaluate What's Working – Clarify Your Core**
   Don't multiply everything; only multiply what's producing fruit. Ask:
   - What do I do best?
   - What generates the most fruit?
   - What can I do that no one else can?

   Then, build around that core.

2. **Systemize the Repeatable**
   If something works, make it teachable. Systems create scalability.
   - Write down your process.
   - Create checklists.
   - Automate tasks.
   - Train someone to do it.

   What you can document, you can duplicate. If you can't repeat it, you can't multiply it.

3. **Build a Team, Not Just a Task List – Delegate What You Don't Need to Do**
   You can't multiply alone. Wisdom knows what to release so you can focus on what brings results. Invest in people who can carry the mission.
   - Delegate authority, not just assignments.
   - Equip and empower, don't micromanage.
   - Hire character and teach skills.

4. **Measure What Matters**
   Track progress, review results, and celebrate wins. Use dashboards, milestones, and key performance indicators (KPIs)—not for pressure, but for **clarity on progress.** Spend your energy, time, and finances in alignment with your goals and objectives related to your assignment.

5. **Pray Before You Push**
   Just because you're capable of scaling something doesn't mean you should yet. **Ask the Lord:**
   - "Is now the time?"
   - "Is this the area?"
   - "Who do I need with me?"
   - "Where am I blind?"

It's wise to involve the Holy Spirit in every decision because multiplication and scaling aren't magic; they begin with spiritual momentum built on strategic obedience.

SECTION 6. **Reflection Questions**

1. What talent, skill, or opportunity have I buried out of fear or neglect?
   - What has God placed in my hands that I haven't fully used?

2. Have I mistaken faithfulness for playing it safe?
   - Where have I been playing it safe instead of multiplying with faith?

3. What can I begin multiplying today with focus and faith?
   - What part of my life or work needs a multiplication strategy?

4. Where do I need systems, support, or mentorship to scale wisely?
   - Who can I learn from to scale wisely and steward growth?

SECTION 7. **Prayer Declaration**

Father, I thank You for entrusting me with time, resources, gifts, and relationships. I refuse to bury what You've given me. I repent for every excuse and fear I've partnered with. I ask for wisdom, courage, and discipline to multiply what's in my hand. Teach me to multiply with faith, courage, and wisdom. Let my work bring increase, my systems bring order, and my efforts bring fruit. I declare that I am not just a manager—I am a multiplier. In Jesus' name, amen.

KEY FIVE

GRATITUDE

(What You Express with Your Heart)

Chapter 5.1

The Power of Gratitude

Scripture Focus:
1 Thessalonians 5:18, Psalm 100:4, Luke 17:11–19

1 Thessalonians 5:18 (KJV) *18 In every thing give thanks: for this is the will of God in Christ Jesus concerning you.*

Psalms 100:4 (KJV) *4 Enter into his gates with thanksgiving, and into his courts with praise: be thankful unto him, and bless his name.*

Luke 17:11-19 (KJV) 11 And it came to pass, as he went to Jerusalem, that he passed through the midst of Samaria and Galilee. 12 And as he entered into a certain village, there met him ten men that were lepers, which stood afar off: 13 And they lifted up their voices, and said, Jesus, Master, have mercy on us. 14 And when he saw them, he said unto them, Go shew yourselves unto the priests. And it came to pass, that, as they went, they were cleansed. 15 And one of them, when he saw that he was healed, turned back, and with a loud voice glorified God, 16 And fell down on his face at his feet, giving him thanks: and he was a Samaritan. 17 And Jesus answering said, Were there not ten cleansed? but where are the nine? 18 There are not found that returned to give glory to God, save this stranger. 19 And he said unto him, Arise, go thy way: thy faith hath made thee whole.

INTRODUCTION. Gratitude Is a Gateway

Gratitude is not a personality trait; it's a **spiritual posture**. In the Kingdom, gratitude is not just a "good attitude;" it's a **powerful principle** that governs access, perspective, and joy.

"Give thanks in all circumstances; for this is God's will for you in Christ Jesus." — 1 Thessalonians 5:18

Notice that Paul doesn't say, *"Give thanks for all things,"* but rather, *"in all things."*

Why? Because God isn't asking us to be fake or deny pain. He's calling us to trust Him **above our pain**, to respond with **faith instead of frustration** and **thanksgiving instead of bitterness.**

Gratitude is not just a feeling; it's a **spiritual strategy.** It's a deliberate and conscious choice to focus on the good, even amid challenges. It protects your perspective, aligns your heart with the Kingdom, and prepares you to receive more.

Gratitude is the will of God, not because He needs it but because **we do.**

Gratitude:
- Shifts your focus from lack to provision
- Reframe your pain through the lens of God's faithfulness
- Protects your heart from entitlement, bitterness, and depression
- Makes space for more blessings

Gratitude as a Stewardship Key:
- **Acknowledges** that God is your source
- **Activates** joy and peace
- **Attracts** more favor and breakthrough
- **Alerts** your soul that God is still at work

When you express gratitude, you are **aligning your heart with the Kingdom of God's perspective.**

In this chapter, we'll discover how gratitude:
- Opens doors in the Spirit
- Positions your heart to sustain blessing
- Makes what you have enough until God multiplies it

This chapter will also help you:
- See the hidden power of giving thanks
- Develop a daily gratitude rhythm
- Shift the atmosphere of your home, team, or business with one word: *thanks*

Because **grateful stewards are trustworthy stewards who don't just endure life; they transform it.**

SECTION 1. Psalm 100—Enter with Thanksgiving

"Enter his gates with thanksgiving and his courts with praise; give thanks to him and praise his name." — Psalm 100:4

In the Old Testament, the Tabernacle had gates, courts, and an inner sanctuary. Worshippers had to **enter the outer gates first**, and the protocol was clear: **they were to start with thanksgiving.**

Why does God insist we come to Him this way?

Because gratitude is the **key to access.**

You don't walk into the presence of a King with complaints and demands; you walk in with honor, appreciation, and acknowledgment.

God's presence isn't casual, and gratitude is how we **unlock proximity.**

Thanksgiving is a Gate:
- It opens the door to joy (Psalm 16:11)
- It invites peace into chaos (Philippians 4:6–7)
- It ushers us from survival mode into an overflow mindset
- It realigns our hearts with the truth of who God is

When you say, "Thank You," even when things aren't perfect, you're **telling your soul:**
- "God is still worthy."
- "My story isn't over."
- "He's done it before, and He'll do it again."

Gratitude doesn't change God; **it changes you and enlarges your capacity to receive more.** It's a transformative force that can shift your perspective from one of lack to one of abundance and from despair to hope.

Gratitude is not just a spiritual practice; it's a practical tool for cultivating a positive outlook. It can shift the atmosphere in your home, strengthen your team's culture, and open your heart to **see the good** that God is doing right now.

Complaining closes doors, but gratitude opens **gates**. It's a transformative force that can shift your perspective from one of lack to one of abundance and from despair to hope.

SECTION 2. **Luke 17—The One Who Came Back**

"Jesus asked, 'Were not all ten cleansed? Where are the other nine? Has no one returned to give praise to God except this foreigner?' Then he said to him, 'Rise and go; your faith has made you well.'" — Luke 17:17–19

Jesus healed **ten lepers**—a life-altering, destiny-shifting miracle. Yet **only one** returned to say thank You.

And Jesus notices.

He didn't say, *"That's okay, as long as they're grateful in their hearts."* He asked, *"Where are the others?"*

Gratitude must be **expressed** to be truly **complete**.

This one man received something **the others didn't**:

- They were **healed**.
- He was made **whole**.

In Greek, the word translated as "made well" (*sozo*) also means saved, restored, and made complete.

Gratitude didn't just honor Jesus—it unlocked **wholeness**.

What Does This Teach Us?

- **Gratitude brings you back into the presence of Jesus.** The others moved on; the grateful one moved closer.
- **Gratitude distinguishes you.** While others forget, the thankful stand out.
- **Gratitude multiplies what you've received.** Healing was a gift; wholeness was the reward for honor.

Gratitude is not just a polite gesture; it's a return trip to the Giver. And those who return receive more, not just in material blessings, but in spiritual growth and understanding.

The other nine missed their moment of intimacy. They received the miracle but missed the **Master** and the opportunity to deepen their spiritual connection.

Many people receive provision and answers from God, but never go deeper when they don't come back to say, Thank You.

Gratitude always brings you back, and God always meets you there.

SECTION 3. Gratitude as a Weapon and a Witness

Gratitude doesn't just feel good—it **fights back**.

> *"Do not be anxious about anything, but in every situation, by prayer and petition, with thanksgiving, present your requests to God..."* — Philippians 4:6

Paul doesn't tell us to fight anxiety with positivity. He tells us to fight it with **prayer, petition, and thanksgiving.**

Gratitude Is a Weapon Against:
- **Worry** – You remind yourself of what God has already done
- **Envy** – You stop focusing on what others have
- **Entitlement** – You shift from *"I deserve"* to *"I am blessed"*
- **Negativity** – You replace complaining with celebrating

Gratitude becomes your defense system; it's how you **guard your joy** and **protect your focus.**

When you begin to thank God for what *is*, your mind starts to release what *isn't*. You can't worry and worship at the same time.

But gratitude isn't just a weapon—it's also a **witness**.

When you live with a grateful spirit:
- People notice
- Environments shift
- Teams get healthier
- Marriages grow stronger
- Children become more secure
- Clients, congregants, and coworkers are drawn in

Grateful people carry the fragrance of the Kingdom of God.

And here's the best part: you don't have to feel grateful to **be** grateful. You choose it. You declare it. You practice it. And over time, it rewires your heart.

Gratitude may not always alter your circumstances, but it changes you.

SECTION 4. Building a Lifestyle of Thanksgiving

Gratitude isn't just something you practice when something good happens. It's a **way of life**—a posture you cultivate every day, regardless of how you feel.

> *"Bless the Lord, O my soul, and forget not all his benefits…"* — Psalm 103:2

David talked to his soul. He commanded it to remember. Why? Because **gratitude is a discipline before it becomes a delight.**

Here are five ways to make gratitude a lifestyle:

1. **Start and End Your Day with Thanksgiving**
   Before you scroll, sigh, or stress—say thank You.
   - Thank God for breath.
   - For peace.
   - For access to His presence.
   - For another day to reflect His glory.

   Even five seconds of gratitude can reset your soul.

2. **Keep a Gratitude Journal**
   Every day, write down three things you're thankful for. They can be big or small answers to prayer, unexpected kindness, or the strength to tackle complex tasks.
   You'll start to realize that **God is more involved in your life than you think.**

3. **Thank People Out Loud**
   Gratitude that stays silent serves no one. Express thanks to your loved ones, team, or pastor. Let them know why you're thankful for them. A simple text, a call, or a few words can make a world of difference.
   Gratitude multiplies when it's spoken.

4. **Use Worship as Gratitude Training**
   Worship isn't just emotional; it's an **intentional act of thanksgiving.** Songs that declare who God is and what He's done **train your soul to celebrate instead of complaining.**
5. **Practice Gratitude in the Middle of Pain**
   This one's the hardest, but it's the most powerful.
   - Thank Him for being with you in it
   - Thank Him that He's working all things for good
   - Thank Him that this valley is temporary
   - Thank Him that He hasn't changed, even when everything else has

The most mature stewards can say "Thank You" in a storm.
And when you do? You're walking in trust, authority, and spiritual maturity.

SECTION 5. Reflection Questions

1. Do I express gratitude regularly, or do I mainly focus on what's missing?
2. What are three blessings I've received recently that I haven't thanked God for?
3. Who in my life do I need to thank today?
4. How can I incorporate a daily rhythm of thanksgiving into my home or work life?
5. What area of my life feels the most difficult to be grateful for right now, and what truth from God's Word can I declare over it?

SECTION 6. Prayer Declaration

Father, I thank You—not just for what You've done, but for who You are. I repent for every moment I've focused more on what I lacked than on Your faithful provision. Teach me to be a grateful steward. Train my heart to recognize Your hand in all things. I thank You for the breath in my lungs, the purpose in my life, and the grace that covers me daily. I declare that I am full of joy, faith, and thanksgiving. Anchor my heart in gratitude, and my mouth will declare Your goodness every day. In Jesus' name, amen.

Chapter 5.2

Gratitude Unlocks the Supernatural

Scripture Focus:
John 6:11, John 11:41–44, Philippians 4:6–7, Psalm 50:23

John 6:11 (KJV) *11 And Jesus took the loaves; and when he had given thanks, he distributed to the disciples, and the disciples to them that were set down; and likewise of the fishes as much as they would.*

John 11:41-44 (KJV) *41 Then they took away the stone from the place where the dead was laid. And Jesus lifted up his eyes, and said, Father, I thank thee that thou hast heard me. 42 And I knew that thou hearest me always: but because of the people which stand by I said it, that they may believe that thou hast sent me. 43 And when he thus had spoken, he cried with a loud voice, Lazarus, come forth. 44 And he that was dead came forth, bound hand and foot with graveclothes: and his face was bound about with a napkin. Jesus saith unto them, Loose him, and let him go.*

Philippians 4:6-7 (KJV) *6 Be careful for nothing; but in every thing by prayer and supplication with thanksgiving let your requests be made known unto God. 7 And the peace of God, which passeth all understanding, shall keep your hearts and minds through Christ Jesus.*

Psalms 50:23 (KJV) *23 Whoso offereth praise glorifieth me: and to him that ordereth his conversation aright will I shew the salvation of God.*

INTRODUCTION. Thanksgiving Precedes Power

Gratitude isn't just polite—it's **prophetic**. It's a spiritual principle that, when practiced, can bring about supernatural manifestations in your life.

In Scripture, **thanksgiving is often the trigger for miraculous release.** It is a divine principle that demonstrates alignment with the Kingdom and expectation for God to move.

"Jesus then took the loaves, gave thanks, and distributed..." — John 6:11

"Then Jesus looked up and said, 'Father, I thank You that You have heard me...'" — John 11:41

In both cases, Jesus **gave thanks before the miracle happened.**
- In John 6, the loaves were still **not enough** when He gave thanks.
- In John 11, Lazarus was still **in the tomb** when He gave thanks.

That means **thanksgiving isn't a reaction to the supernatural—it's a setup for it.**

Gratitude unlocks:
- Provision before multiplication
- Breakthrough before resurrection
- Peace before the answer
- Joy before the circumstances change

In this chapter, we'll explore how gratitude is:
- A posture that activates supernatural flow
- A practical tool to resist doubt and anxiety
- A prophetic declaration of trust in advance

Because if you want to live in the supernatural, you must learn how to give thanks **before you see it.**

SECTION 1. Jesus Gave Thanks Before the Miracle

Gratitude is not just something Jesus recommended; it's something He modeled in the most pressure-filled moments of His life.

"Jesus then took the loaves, gave thanks, and distributed to those who were seated as much as they wanted..." — John 6:11

This miracle, the feeding of the five thousand, was a masterclass in supernatural stewardship. Jesus held what **looked like not enough** in His hands. A boy's lunch. Five loaves. Two fish.

The crowd was hungry. The disciples, in their panic, saw the resources as insufficient.

And what did Jesus do?

He **gave thanks.**

He didn't pray for more. He didn't complain about the little. He didn't panic under pressure.

He lifted lack and **blessed it.** And in that moment, the supernatural was triggered. The food didn't multiply in the basket; it multiplied **in the distribution.** As they gave it away, it grew.

Gratitude activates what logic disqualifies.

Jesus showed us that gratitude was the key to **unlocking** the provision.

He modeled that thanksgiving proves **trust in the Father,** and **trust releases the power of God.**

SECTION 2. Gratitude as a Catalyst for Multiplication

We often pray for God to **multiply** our resources. But the question is: Have we **thanked Him** for what we already have?

> *"The one who offers thanksgiving as his sacrifice glorifies me; to one who orders his way rightly I will show the salvation of God."* — Psalm 50:23

This verse links **gratitude with revelation.** When you thank God for what's in your hand, He reveals what's in **His.**

Multiplication doesn't start with hustle—it begins with **honor.**

Here's how gratitude multiplies:

1. **Gratitude multiplies your perspective.**
   You stop saying, *"It's not enough,"* and start saying, *"Thank You for this seed."* That shift alone moves you from a state of lack to one of expectation.

2. **Gratitude multiplies your capacity.**
   A grateful heart carries more peace, joy, creativity, and resilience. You become a better leader, parent, builder, or team member.
3. **Gratitude multiplies your favor.**
   People gravitate to those who carry a spirit of thankfulness. Doors open for the humble and the honorable.
4. **Gratitude multiplies your influence.**
   When you speak with gratitude—about your team, your clients, your family—it elevates the culture around you. Gratitude reproduces itself in others.
   What you bless, God multiplies. What you curse, you shrink.
   Jesus blessed the bread **before** it looked like a miracle, and that moment of honor released the Kingdom's economy to feed the five thousand.
   Never underestimate the power of a "Thank You." It could be the difference between maintaining and multiplying.

SECTION 3. Gratitude Defies Natural Logic

Gratitude, often perceived as a response to receiving something, doesn't always make sense in the context of anticipation, and that's the point.

When Jesus thanked the Father **before** Lazarus came out of the tomb, the people around Him were still grieving. Lazarus was in a sealed grave, and the situation looked final.

> *"So they took away the stone. Then Jesus looked up and said, 'Father, I thank you that you have heard me.'"* — John 11:41

No one else saw a miracle coming, but Jesus was already **thanking God for the answer He hadn't seen yet.**

That's supernatural thinking.

Why Is This Important?

Because natural thinking waits until:
- The bills are paid
- The healing manifests
- The opportunity comes
- The door opens

But supernatural gratitude thanks God in advance.
It says:
- "Even if I don't see it yet, I believe You're moving."
- "Even when I'm still waiting, You are still worthy."
- "Even when it looks like lack, You are my Source."

Gratitude in advance is one of the most explicit **acts of faith**.

You're not thanking God for what He's done. You're thanking Him because you trust what He's about to do.

And that kind of faith shifts atmospheres. It brings peace in the middle of storms and clarity in the middle of confusion.

It invites the supernatural—not because you earned it, but because your posture said: **"I trust You anyway.**

SECTION 4. Giving Thanks in Advance

Gratitude in advance is the language of expectation. It's one thing to be thankful **after** the breakthrough. It's another to thank God **before** the door opens, the healing manifests, or the need is met.

Being thankful before you see the manifestation is the kind of faith that:
- Pleases God (Hebrews 11:6)
- Moves mountains (Mark 11:23–24)
- Ushers in peace (Philippians 4:6–7)
- Positions you to receive answers with boldness (James 1:6)

"Do not be anxious about anything, but in everything, by prayer and petition, with thanksgiving, present your requests to God." — Philippians 4:6

This Scripture doesn't just say *pray*; it says pray **with thanksgiving**. When you pair your requests with gratitude, you're saying:
- "I trust You more than I trust what I see."
- "I believe You're working even in silence."
- "I know who You are, so I can thank You before I hold the answer."

Gratitude in Advance Looks Like:
- Thanking God for healing before your body feels different
- Thanking God for provision before the check arrives

- Thanking God for wisdom before the situation makes sense
- Thanking God for open doors before any have opened

This kind of thanksgiving makes Hell nervous because it's a declaration that **your confidence is in God, not in outcomes.**

When you thank Him in advance:
- Your soul stabilizes
- Your spirit strengthens
- Your mindset shifts
- Your heart prepares to receive

Thanksgiving is not the finish line. It's the starting gun. It launches you into a supernatural partnership with the Kingdom.

SECTION 5. **Building a Gratitude-Driven Lifestyle**

The supernatural isn't something you visit occasionally. It's something you live in **when gratitude becomes your way of life.**

When you stop treating thankfulness like a moment and start treating it like a **mindset**, everything changes.

"Rejoice always, pray continually, give thanks in all circumstances..."
— 1 Thessalonians 5:16–18

Notice Paul doesn't say to *feel thankful*. He says to *give thanks* because gratitude is a **choice**, not a condition.

Here's how to build that lifestyle:

1. **Speak It Daily**
   Don't wait for the "big blessings." Start your day by saying, *"Thank You, God, for breath, peace, mercy, and opportunity."*
   The more you say it, the more you believe it. The more you know it, the more you see it.

2. **Saturate Your Space with Praise**
   Fill your car, home, and headphones with worship that lifts your heart in gratitude.
   This atmosphere is hostile to anxiety and confusion.

3. **Thank Before You Think**
   Whenever something frustrates you, pause and find **one thing** to thank God for in the middle of it.
   It won't fix the problem immediately, but it will fix your perspective, and that's where the miracle begins.

4. **Thank God in Conversations**
   Instead of venting or worrying out loud, practice saying,
   "I don't know how this will work out, but I'm grateful God is working."
   That single sentence can shift the room.

5. **Model Gratitude in Your Family or Team**
   Make "Thank You" the culture. Publicly celebrate wins. Acknowledge people's value. Thank those you lead and thank those who lead you.
   Gratitude multiplies when you model it.

Why This Matters

Gratitude keeps:
- Your heart tender
- Your mouth aligned
- Your faith active
- Your spirit expectant

And this combination invites the **supernatural** daily.

SECTION 6. Reflection Questions

1. Have I been waiting to see the miracle before expressing gratitude?
2. What situation in my life right now needs a shift in perspective through thanksgiving?
3. How can I begin giving thanks in advance, even before the changes occur?
4. What small blessings have I overlooked that God is waiting for me to honor?
5. Where can I model gratitude better in my home, workplace, or ministry?

SECTION 7. **Prayer Declaration**

Father, I thank You not just for what You've done, but for what You're doing, even when I can't see it. I repent for every moment I've chosen worry over worship and fear over faith. I declare that I trust You in advance. I give You thanks now for the doors that are opening, the healing that is manifesting, the favor that is coming, and the breakthrough that's in motion. Teach me to walk in daily gratitude and let my heart remain full of praise, no matter what I face. In Jesus' name, amen.

Chapter 5.3

The Overflow of a Grateful Heart

Scripture Focus:
Luke 6:45, Proverbs 4:23, Psalm 23:5,
2 Corinthians 4:15

Luke 6:45 (KJV) *45 A good man out of the good treasure of his heart bringeth forth that which is good; and an evil man out of the evil treasure of his heart bringeth forth that which is evil: for of the abundance of the heart his mouth speaketh.*

Proverbs 4:23 (KJV) *23 Keep thy heart with all diligence; for out of it are the issues of life.*

Psalms 23:5 (KJV) *5 Thou preparest a table before me in the presence of mine enemies: thou anointest my head with oil; my cup runneth over.*

2 Corinthians 4:15 (KJV) *15 For all things are for your sakes, that the abundant grace might through the thanksgiving of many redound to the glory of God.*

INTRODUCTION. What Fills, Spills

Gratitude is not just a reaction—it's a **resource** that fills a spiritual **reservoir**.

Whatever fills your heart will eventually **spill out of your mouth, your choices, your responses, and your relationships.** Jesus put it this way:

"Out of the abundance of the heart his mouth speaks." — Luke 6:45

That means gratitude is not something you do occasionally; it's something you **carry internally**. When your heart is full of thanksgiving, everything in your life begins to reflect it:
- Your words become encouraging
- Your prayers become bold
- Your relationships become peaceful
- Your leadership becomes life-giving

A grateful heart doesn't just survive; it **overflows**.
This chapter will help you:
- Understand the spiritual law of overflow
- Identify what's leaking from your heart
- Learn how to fill your life with thanksgiving until it becomes your atmosphere

Because gratitude was never meant to be seasonal—it's meant to be a source of **continual overflow**.

SECTION 1. The Heart Is a Well

"Above all else, guard your heart, for everything you do flows from it." — Proverbs 4:23 (NIV)

Your heart is not just an organ—it's a **spiritual reservoir**.
Everything you say, decide, lead, and pursue flows from **what's inside** your heart. If it's full of fear, fear comes out. If it's full of frustration, frustration spills out.
But if it's full of **gratitude**?
Then joy flows. Patience flows. Peace flows. Encouragement flows. Hope flows.
That's why gratitude isn't about moments—it's about **maintenance**.
You don't build a thankful life by reacting to blessings; you create it by **guarding and filling your heart daily**.
Jesus said that the mouth reveals the heart's overflow. So, if your speech is full of sarcasm, stress, negativity, or complaint, it's not just a vocal issue; it's a **heart issue**.
How to Guard the Well of Your Heart:
- Watch what you allow in (conversations, content, and complaints)

- Keep a running list of God's faithfulness
- Journal daily wins or answered prayers
- Turn delays and detours into declarations of trust
- Surround yourself with grateful voices

A heart that's protected and filled becomes a fountain, not a drain.

SECTION 2. Gratitude Flows Where It's Stored

Paul writes to the church at Corinth:

> *"All of this is for your benefit, so that the grace that is reaching more and more people may cause thanksgiving to overflow to the glory of God."* — 2 Corinthians 4:15

Overflow doesn't start with circumstances; it begins with **grace.**

Paul had been beaten, shipwrecked, and falsely accused—and yet, he says **thanksgiving is still overflowing.** Why? Because he anchored his heart in something deeper than his conditions.

Overflow Happens When:
- You **choose to focus** on what God has done
- You **practice gratitude** even when it's hard
- You **let grace define** your perspective
- You **intentionally create rhythms** that feed your thankfulness

Your external life will eventually reflect your internal posture. If you want peace and praise to flow freely, you must regularly **pour in gratitude.**

You can't overflow with what you've never stored.

Make deposits of gratitude daily. The returns will change your mindset, your marriage, your money, and your ministry.

SECTION 3. A Grateful Life Becomes a Giving Life

Gratitude doesn't stay internal; it becomes an **external expression.**

> *"You anoint my head with oil; my cup overflows."* — Psalm 23:5

David didn't say, *"My cup is full."* He said, *"It overflows."* Why? Because **God doesn't just fill you for you—He fills you to pour out.**

When your heart is full of thanksgiving:
- You become a **blessing** to others
- You speak **life**, not just encouragement
- You sow with **joy**, not guilt
- You lead with **abundance**, not survival

The Overflow of Gratitude Produces:

1. **Generosity**
   Grateful people give more freely of their time, talents, and treasures. They know everything they have is a gift, so they hold it with open hands.

   "Freely you have received; freely give." — Matthew 10:8

   When you know how much grace you've received, it becomes easy to **become a conduit** of that grace.

2. **Encouragement**
   When you're overflowing with thanksgiving, you're quick to affirm others. You see the best. You celebrate small wins. You speak life into tired places.
   This overflow transforms relationships, teams, marriages, and ministries.

3. **Excellence**
   Gratitude fuels effort. When you're thankful for the opportunity, you show up differently. You prepare. You stay late. You don't grumble. You **glorify**.

4. **Compassion**
   Gratitude keeps your heart soft toward others. Instead of comparing or criticizing, you **bless** and **build**.

5. **Stability**
   When your heart is grounded in thanksgiving, you don't allow trends or circumstances to affect you. You carry peace in the storm, and people want to anchor near you.
   Overflow isn't just for you—it's how God meets others through you.

When your life is rooted in gratitude, your entire posture changes. Your house becomes a haven. Your business becomes a blessing. Your calling becomes a conduit.

SECTION 4. Gratitude That Sustains Through Every Season

Gratitude gives you **spiritual stamina.** When you keep your heart filled with thankfulness, you don't just rise with blessing; you stand in trials.

> *"Though the fig tree does not bud and there are no grapes on the vines... yet I will rejoice in the Lord."* — Habakkuk 3:17–18

Habakkuk didn't rejoice **because** everything was perfect. He rejoiced **despite** everything falling apart.

A heart that can overflow with gratitude **in the wilderness**, not just in the harvest, is what spiritual maturity looks like.

Gratitude in Dry Seasons:
- **Keeps you from quitting.** When you thank God for past victories, it reminds you that He's still with you now.
- **Changes how you pray.** Instead of begging God out of desperation, you approach Him with faith-filled expectations.
- **Protects your perspective.** You stop magnifying the problem and start magnifying the Promise Keeper.
- **Strengthens your endurance.** Gratitude reminds your soul: "We've been here before. He brought us out then. He'll do it again."

Gratitude is not denial. It's defiance against discouragement.
You're not ignoring reality; you're confronting it with truth.

SECTION 5. Building a Culture of Overflow

Gratitude is contagious. When it overflows from your life, it doesn't just change your story; it changes your **surroundings.**

As a leader, whether in a family, a business, a church, or a team, you hold the reins in creating a **culture**—an environment shaped by values.

And there's no more powerful value than **overflowing gratitude.**

How to Build a Culture of Overflow:

1. **Model It Openly**
   Let people hear you say "Thank You" to God and others. Visible gratitude becomes a pattern others follow.

2. **Celebrate Progress, Not Just Perfection**
   A culture of gratitude values the journey. It celebrates growth, not just goals. Milestones, small wins, and breakthroughs—all are acknowledged.

3. **Honor People Publicly**
   Call out excellence. Highlight unseen effort. Send notes of thanks. Acknowledge what people bring, and they'll bring more of it.

4. **Tell Stories of God's Faithfulness**
   Regularly rehearse your testimonies at home, in your workplace, or at church. Let thankfulness become the soundtrack of your culture.
   What you honor, you multiply.

If you want to lead people into supernatural living, don't just teach miracles—**model gratitude.**

Overflowing gratitude creates an atmosphere where:
- Faith rises
- Cynicism melts
- Joy spreads
- The Holy Spirit feels welcome

Your culture starts with your confession.

SECTION 6. Reflection Questions

1. What's been overflowing from my heart lately—gratitude or grumbling?
2. What regular habit can I build to keep my heart filled with thanksgiving?
3. How has gratitude influenced the people around me?
4. What dry season am I walking through that needs a gratitude reset?
5. How can I foster a culture of gratitude in my home, ministry, or workplace?

SECTION 7. **Prayer Declaration**

Father, thank You for every good gift. I choose to guard my heart and fill it with thanksgiving. I refuse to let complaint or fear take root in my spirit. Instead, I overflow with Your goodness. I thank You in every season—when I see the miracle and when I'm still waiting. I declare that my life is a well of gratitude, my words carry encouragement, and my influence releases joy. Let my heart be so full of thanks that it touches everyone around me. In Jesus' name, amen.

KEY SIX

PRUDENCE

(What You Do with Your Time)

Chapter 6.1

Redeeming the Time

Scripture Focus:
Ephesians 5:15–17, Psalm 90:12, Ecclesiastes 3:1

Ephesians 5:15-17 (KJV) *15 See then that ye walk circumspectly, not as fools, but as wise, 16 Redeeming the time, because the days are evil. 17 Wherefore be ye not unwise, but understanding what the will of the Lord is.*

Psalms 90:12 (KJV) *12 So teach us to number our days, that we may apply our hearts unto wisdom.*

Ecclesiastes 3:1 (KJV) *1 To every thing there is a season, and a time to every purpose under the heaven:*

INTRODUCTION. Time Is a Stewardship Test

Time is not just a schedule; it's a **sacred trust**. It's the only resource you can't get more of, buy back, or delay.

> *"Look carefully then how you walk, not as unwise but as wise, making the best use of the time, because the days are evil."* — Ephesians 5:15–16 (ESV)

Paul's counsel is not just about managing time but about doing so with a sense of urgency and wisdom. It's about avoiding distractions, delays, and dead-end thinking. Because how you use your time reflects what you value, believe, and expect from God.

Time stewardship is not merely about filling your schedule with tasks; **it's about being intentional in your actions.**

This chapter will help you:
- Reframe time as a Kingdom asset
- Identify where time is leaking from your life

- Learn to walk in Spirit-led urgency, not anxiety
- Align your schedule with your purpose

Because when you **redeem the time**, you don't just make better plans—you fulfill divine assignments.

SECTION 1. Numbering Your Days for Wisdom

"Teach us to number our days, that we may gain a heart of wisdom."
— Psalm 90:12

This prayer from Moses is more than poetic—it's prophetic. To **number your days** doesn't just mean to count them. It means **valuing** them, **prioritizing** them, and **using them with intention.**

Living intentionally is not just a concept; it's a way of life that aligns your actions with your divine purpose.

Most people act as if time is unlimited. But wisdom says: **"You don't have time to waste."**

What Does Numbering Your Days Look Like?
- Asking daily: *"What matters most today?"*
- Refusing to give energy to what doesn't bear fruit
- Saying no to distractions, even good ones, that pull you from your divine purpose
- Structuring your time around God's voice, not others' demands

Wisdom is knowing that **everything has a time, but not everything is worth your time.**

"There is a time for everything, and a season for every activity under the heavens..." — Ecclesiastes 3:1

If you don't define your time, the world will do it for you. Culture will fill your calendar. Urgency will replace purpose, and you'll spend your life busy but **not fruitful.**

God wants His people to live **wise and well-timed lives**, not reactive ones.

SECTION 2. The Cost of Wasted Time

Time is the currency of life. Once you spend it, you never get it back.

That's why the enemy doesn't always need to destroy you; he just needs to **distract** you. If he can keep you procrastinating, over-committed, or endlessly "waiting for the right time," he's already won.

Wasted time often disguises itself as rest, delay, or preparation.
Signs You're Wasting Time:
- You're endlessly preparing but never launching
- You say yes to everything and end up doing nothing well
- You keep postponing obedience until you "feel ready"
- You spend more time reacting than planning

But here's the good news:
Although time is limited, **God redeems it.**

"I will restore to you the years that the locust has eaten..." — Joel 2:25

Even if you've wasted years, God can accelerate your growth, multiply your impact, and redeem the lost moments.

But it starts with **owning your time.**

When you take responsibility for your time, you step into **a new level of spiritual authority.**

SECTION 3. Walking in Spirit-Led Time

"The steps of a good man are ordered by the Lord..." — Psalm 37:23

There's a difference between **managing your time** and **being led in your time.**

Time stewardship in the Kingdom is not just about planning; it's about **alignment.** Many people fill their calendars with obligations and opportunities, but never ask, *"God, is this from You?"*

The wise steward asks:
- "Where should I invest my energy today?"
- "What assignment is for now, and what's for later?"
- "What am I doing under pressure instead of out of purpose?"

Spirit-led time management means your calendar becomes a canvas for divine movement.

Walking in God's Timing Means:
- You say no without guilt
- You say yes without hesitation
- You trust His pace, not your pressure
- You flow in peace, not panic
- You recognize that *"later"* can be as disobedient as *"never"*

Sometimes, delay is disobedience dressed as wisdom. And sometimes rest is obedience that feels like resistance to culture.

When your time belongs to God, your life becomes a reflection of **peaceful precision.**

SECTION 4. Resetting Your Rhythms

If your life feels out of control, your rhythms probably are.

Time stewardship requires **intentional structure**, not rigid routines that squeeze out the Spirit—but rhythms that create **space for God's best.**

> *"Six days you shall labor, but on the seventh day you shall rest..."* — Exodus 34:21

Even in the law, God built in rhythms of work and rest. Why? Because God knew your **fruitfulness depends on your flow.**

5 Time-Stewardship Rhythms to Establish

1. **Morning Focus Time**
   Start your day with clarity—word, worship, and priorities. Your first 30 minutes can set the course for 12 hours of peace.

2. **Weekly Planning**
   Don't let weeks "just happen." Review your priorities on Sunday or Monday. Ask:
   - What's mission-critical this week?
   - Where's my energy needed most?

3. **Strategic No's**
   Learn to decline opportunities that don't align with your assignment. You're not being unkind. **You're being clear** and empowering yourself to focus on what truly matters.

4. **Sabbath Rhythm**
   Choose one day to unplug, recharge, reflect, and worship. The Sabbath isn't a restriction; it's a gift.

5. **End-of-Day Reset**
   Take 10 minutes to review wins, identify loose ends, and thank God. This closes the day in peace, not stress.

   Healthy rhythms redeem time automatically because they eliminate waste and protect margin.

   Stewards don't just ask, *"What should I be doing?"* They ask, *"When should I be doing it, and at what pace?"*

SECTION 5. Reflection Questions

1. Where have I been spending time that isn't producing fruit?
2. What tasks or commitments am I holding onto out of fear or guilt?
3. What is one area of my life that needs a more precise rhythm or boundary?
4. When was the last time I invited the Holy Spirit into my weekly planning?
5. How can I better reflect Kingdom values in how I use my time each day?

SECTION 6. Prayer Declaration

Father, I thank You for the gift of time. I repent for the moments I've wasted in fear, distraction, or delay. Teach me to walk in Your timing. Help me to number my days, to live with purpose, and to steward my schedule with wisdom. I declare that I align my time with the Kingdom. I walk in divine rhythm, Spirit-led assignments, and Kingdom clarity. I do not chase the urgent. I pursue what matters. In Jesus' name, amen.

Chapter 6.2

The Wisdom of Scheduling

Scripture Focus:
Proverbs 21:5, Luke 14:28–30, 1 Corinthians 14:40

Proverbs 21:5 (KJV) *5 The thoughts of the diligent tend only to plenteousness; but of every one that is hasty only to want.*

Luke 14:28-30 (KJV) *28 For which of you, intending to build a tower, sitteth not down first, and counteth the cost, whether he have sufficient to finish it? 29 Lest haply, after he hath laid the foundation, and is not able to finish it, all that behold it begin to mock him, 30 Saying, This man began to build, and was not able to finish.*

1 Corinthians 14:40 (KJV) *40 Let all things be done decently and in order.*

INTRODUCTION. Your Schedule Is a Spiritual Statement

Your calendar reveals your calling.

While many view schedules as secular or mechanical, in the Kingdom, a well-crafted schedule is a powerful **spiritual weapon**. It transforms vision into progress, calling into consistency, and purpose into peace.

> "The plans of the diligent lead surely to abundance, but everyone who is hasty comes only to poverty." — Proverbs 21:5

Planning is not a lack of faith—it's **evidence of faith.** It demonstrates your belief that what God has entrusted to you is worth stewarding.

This chapter will help you:
- Align your schedule with your values
- Recognize what needs to be pruned, paused, or prioritized
- Use structure to serve your purpose—not suffocate it
- Create margins that protect your peace and productivity

Because if the enemy can't destroy your calling, he'll try to **disrupt your structure.**

Remember, scheduling wisely is not just an act of stewardship, but also an **act of warfare.** It's a call to action, a battle cry to take control of your life, assignment, and destiny.

SECTION 1. Structure Unlocks Stewardship

"For which of you, desiring to build a tower, does not first sit down and count the cost...?" — Luke 14:28

Jesus praised planning. He was essentially saying, How can you build without calculating? In other words, how can you achieve your goals without first preparing for them?

Many people pray for increase but haven't prepared for it. **Faith prepares.** Faithful stewards don't just dream—they **design, knowing that they will only reach their goals by identifying the steps required and taking them.**

SECTION 2. What Gets Scheduled Gets Done

If it's not on your calendar, it likely won't become a reality.

Whether it's praying more, studying the Word, exercising, or building a ministry, these **desires will remain mere wishes if not scheduled.** Without a commitment on your calendar, they risk being overshadowed by other tasks.

"But everything should be done in a fitting and orderly way." — 1 Corinthians 14:40

Order is a Kingdom principle, and it always comes before increase. From creation to the cross to the early church, God always worked through **design, not disorder.**

Scheduling Brings:
1. **Clarity** — you know what deserves your time
2. **Accountability** — you protect your priorities
3. **Peace** — you stop living in constant reaction mode
4. **Momentum** — small wins compound when repeated with consistency

Keys to Faith-Filled Scheduling:
1. **Plan Around Priorities, Not Pressures:** When Planning Your Schedule, remember to prioritize what's truly important over what's merely urgent. If you always say yes to urgent things, you'll never make time for what's truly important.
2. **Make Time for What Fuels You:** Recharge time isn't selfish—it's stewardship. Schedule spiritual, physical, and emotional renewal.
3. **Batch and Block Your Time:** Group similar tasks together and allocate dedicated time slots on your calendar. Don't let distractions leak in.
4. **Review and Refine Weekly** Spend 15 minutes on Sundays to adjust your plan. Seek guidance from the Holy Spirit: *"Does this reflect my purpose?"*

SECTION 3. Scheduling for Margin and Mission

Margin is the space between your load and your limits. Without margin, you live life exhausted, reactive, and overwhelmed, even when you're doing "good things." By embracing margin, you open the door to a more balanced, intentional, and fulfilling life.

Jesus had a full schedule—but never a frantic one. He demonstrated that it is possible to be fully engaged in life without being overwhelmed.

> *"But Jesus often withdrew to lonely places and prayed."* — Luke 5:16

If the Son of God scheduled solitude, **so should you.**

Scheduling for Margin Means:
- **Leaving space between appointments** so you're not rushing everywhere

- **Scheduling rest and reflection** like you would a meeting
- **Planning buffer days or times** for thinking, vision, or interruptions
- **Ending your day before your body collapses** from burnout

Margin creates room for the **unexpected move of God**.

Without margin, you'll miss divine interruptions, lose your creativity, and live in survival mode instead of stewardship. These divine interruptions, often disguised as unexpected opportunities or challenges, are crucial for your growth and the fulfillment of your mission.

Scheduling for Mission Means:
- Prioritizing what aligns with your God-given assignment
- Protecting your "yes" for fruitful things, not just familiar things
- Using time as a tool to advance Kingdom impact—week by week

When you schedule with the mission in mind, your calendar becomes a canvas of divine purpose.

SECTION 4. The Spirituality of Saying No

Many believers feel guilty saying no. But in Scripture, saying no was often a sign of obedience.
- Jesus said no to the crowds so He could pray.
- Nehemiah said no to distractions so he could finish the wall.
- Paul said no to certain cities because the Spirit led him elsewhere.

Saying no to one thing means saying yes to what matters more.

Every yes has a cost. A cluttered calendar often reveals a **cluttered identity**—someone trying to prove worth through activity.

But wise stewards understand: **No is not rejection; it's redirection.**

How to Say No Spiritually:
- Ask, *"Will this advance my calling or dilute it?"*
- Pray before committing—even to good things
- Remember that pruning is God's strategy for **greater fruitfulness**

"He cuts off every branch in me that bears no fruit..." — John 15:2

Scheduling is pruning in action. And pruning, though painful, protects your future fruit.

SECTION 5. **Reflection Questions**

1. Does my current schedule reflect my values or just my responsibilities?
2. What activities need to be pruned to protect my purpose?
3. Where am I overcommitted out of fear, guilt, or insecurity?
4. How can I build more margin into my calendar this week?
5. What one commitment can I add that aligns with my long-term mission?

SECTION 6. **Prayer Declaration**

Father, thank You for the gift of time and purpose. I surrender my schedule to You. Teach me to steward each hour with intention and grace. I declare that my calendar reflects my calling, not chaos. I say yes to what matters and no to distraction. Let my rhythms produce fruit and protect peace. I walk in wisdom, not pressure. My schedule is Spirit-led and Kingdom-aligned. In Jesus' name, amen.

Chapter 6.3

Time, Seasons, and Discernment

Scripture Focus:
Ecclesiastes 3:1–8, 1 Chronicles 12:32, Galatians 6:9

Ecclesiastes 3:1-8 (KJV) *1 To every thing there is a season, and a time to every purpose under the heaven: 2 A time to be born, and a time to die; a time to plant, and a time to pluck up that which is planted; 3 A time to kill, and a time to heal; a time to break down, and a time to build up; 4 A time to weep, and a time to laugh; a time to mourn, and a time to dance; 5 A time to cast away stones, and a time to gather stones together; a time to embrace, and a time to refrain from embracing; 6 A time to get, and a time to lose; a time to keep, and a time to cast away; 7 A time to rend, and a time to sew; a time to keep silence, and a time to speak; 8 A time to love, and a time to hate; a time of war, and a time of peace.*

1 Chronicles 12:32 (KJV) *32 And of the children of Issachar, which were men that had understanding of the times, to know what Israel ought to do; the heads of them were two hundred; and all their brethren were at their commandment.*

Galatians 6:9 (KJV) *9 And let us not be weary in well doing: for in due season we shall reap, if we faint not.*

INTRODUCTION. It's Not Just About Time—It's About Timing

You can do the right thing at the wrong time and get the wrong result.

In the Kingdom, wisdom is not just knowing **what** to do—it's knowing **when** to do it. That's the difference between **activity** and **anointing**.

"There is a time for everything, and a season for every activity under the heavens." — Ecclesiastes 3:1

Not every opportunity is for now. Not every delay is a denial. Not every open door is a divine door.

That's why discernment is critical.

This chapter will help you:
- Recognize the seasons of your life and purpose
- Discern between movement and momentum
- Avoid premature decisions or prolonged delay
- Submit your timing to God's direction

Because divine stewardship isn't just about using time well—it's about **obeying divine timing**.

SECTION 1. Seasons Require Sensitivity

"The sons of Issachar understood the times and knew what Israel should do." — 1 Chronicles 12:32

This tribe wasn't known for weapons—they were known for **wisdom.** They could discern what season Israel was in and align their decisions accordingly.

This is the call for every Kingdom steward: **Know your time. Move with wisdom. Obey without delay.**

SECTION 2. Delays, Deadlines, and Divine Appointments

In the natural, we plan with deadlines. In the Spirit, God often moves through **divine appointments.**

That's why timing can feel unpredictable, but when you walk with God, it's always **perfect.**

"Let us not grow weary in well-doing, for at the proper time we will reap a harvest if we do not give up." — Galatians 6:9

There is a **proper time.** Not just any time. Not your time. Not their time.

Why Does God Delay?
- To develop **your character**
- To protect you from premature exposure
- To prepare the right connections
- To align spiritual and natural conditions

Delays are often disguised **deliverances.**

God sees the bigger picture. What feels like waiting is often **weaving:** God stitching together pieces you can't see yet.

How to Handle Delay with Discernment:
- Ask, "Is this a test of my **trust** or a cue to move on?"
- Don't force what isn't ready—wait for confirmation
- Stay faithful in what's in front of you
- Worship while you wait—it keeps your heart soft and your spirit alert

God doesn't just redeem time—He **controls** it. He's not late. He's not passive. He's strategic.

Discernment helps you obey in rhythm with Heaven—not in reaction to pressure.

SECTION 3. Discern the Difference Between Good and God

Not every open door is an invitation. Not every opportunity is your assignment.

Discernment says, *"Just because it looks good doesn't mean it's from God."*

"All things are permissible, but not all things are beneficial..." — 1 Corinthians 10:23

Good stewards don't just count minutes—they **measure momentum.** They ask:
- "Is this God's will or my ambition?"
- "Is this wise or just exciting?"
- "Is this opportunity from Heaven—or a distraction dressed as destiny?"

Discernment is how you know when to:
- Launch or wait

- Speak or stay silent
- Plant or prune
- Build or rest

You can't steward time well without a **listening ear** and a **submitted heart**.

SECTION 4. When to Push and When to Pause

One of the greatest marks of maturity is knowing when to move and when to wait.

"There is a time to plant and a time to uproot... a time to search and a time to give up..." — Ecclesiastes 3:2, 6

God works in rhythms, not rush. And walking in wisdom means you learn to **sense divine momentum**, not just respond to emotion.

When to Push:
- When God gives clear instruction
- When the opportunity aligns with long-standing preparation
- When peace confirms the prompting
- When obedience requires urgency

Pushing isn't striving. It's **moving in faith** when the Spirit stirs you.

When to Pause:
- When clarity is missing
- When your soul is anxious
- When wise counsel suggests caution
- When your desire is louder than God's whisper

Pausing isn't quitting—it's preparing. It's giving space for the Holy Spirit to affirm or adjust your direction.

"Be still, and know that I am God." — Psalm 46:10

Some doors only open after you've stopped forcing the handle.

Discernment helps you avoid costly detours and maximize strategic moments. It's not just about what's ahead—it's about walking with God **through every step**.

SECTION 5. **Reflection Questions**

1. What season am I currently in—and what does it require of me?
2. Am I rushing into something that God is asking me to wait on?
3. Where have I confused delay with denial?
4. What recent opportunity needs prayerful discernment before a response?
5. Am I in a planting, pruning, building, or resting season?

SECTION 6. **Prayer Declaration**

Father, I thank You for being the Lord of time and seasons. I trust Your timing over mine. Teach me to move when You say move, and to wait when You say wait. Help me discern the season I'm in, so I can walk in wisdom, not impulse. I declare that I am not led by pressure but by purpose. I steward my time with clarity, and I align my actions with Heaven's rhythm. In Jesus' name, amen.

KEY SEVEN

FORESIGHT

(What You Do with Your Money)

Chapter 7.1

Seeing Money Through Heaven's Eyes

Scripture Focus:
Matthew 6:19–21, Luke 16:10–11,
Deuteronomy 8:18, Proverbs 22:3

Matthew 6:19-21 (KJV) *19 Lay not up for yourselves treasures upon earth, where moth and rust doth corrupt, and where thieves break through and steal: 20 But lay up for yourselves treasures in heaven, where neither moth nor rust doth corrupt, and where thieves do not break through nor steal: 21 For where your treasure is, there will your heart be also.*

Luke 16:10-11 (KJV) *10 He that is faithful in that which is least is faithful also in much: and he that is unjust in the least is unjust also in much. 11 If therefore ye have not been faithful in the unrighteous mammon, who will commit to your trust the true riches?*

Deuteronomy 8:18 (KJV) *18 But thou shalt remember the LORD thy God: for it is he that giveth thee power to get wealth, that he may establish his covenant which he sware unto thy fathers, as it is this day.*

Proverbs 22:3 (KJV) *3 A prudent man foreseeth the evil, and hideth himself: but the simple pass on, and are punished.*

INTRODUCTION. Money Is a Mirror and a Test

Money is not just a medium of exchange; it's a **spiritual indicator**.

> *"For where your treasure is, there your heart will be also."* — Matthew 6:21 (NIV)

This profound verse encapsulates the spiritual essence of money.

Jesus didn't say your treasure follows your heart—He said your **heart follows your treasure, which** means how you handle money reveals what you truly believe, prioritize, and value.

In the Kingdom, money is both a **test** and a **tool**:
- A test of **faithfulness and foresight**
- A tool for **impact and expansion**

God doesn't have a problem with you having money. He doesn't want money having **you**.

This chapter will help you:
- Reframe wealth from a Kingdom perspective
- Recognize financial stewardship as spiritual warfare
- Understand how trust and stewardship, not just tithing, govern your financial future
- Cultivate foresight for financial decisions with lasting fruit

Because **money is not just provision—it's preparation.** It has the power to transform your life and the lives of others, depending on how it's managed.

SECTION 1. Money Is Spiritual, Not Just Practical

Many Christians separate their faith from their finances. **They trust God with their soul but not with their strategy.**

But in Scripture, money is addressed more than prayer, heaven, or hell. Why? Because money touches everything, and how we handle it reveals **who's leading our lives.**

> *"If you have not been trustworthy in handling worldly wealth, who will trust you with true riches?"* — Luke 16:11 (NIV)

Jesus connects **natural money** with **spiritual promotion**. The 'true riches' mentioned in Luke 16:11 refer to the spiritual blessings and rewards that come from faithful stewardship of our worldly wealth.

Money Is Spiritual Because:
- It influences your decisions
- It tests your motives
- It affects your worship
- It reveals your trust
- It impacts your legacy

The enemy knows if he can keep you broke, bound, or blind about money, he can limit your ability to serve, give, build, or go.

That's why understanding money through the Kingdom's lens is not a luxury—it's **a necessity.**

We must stop viewing money as a threat to our faith and start viewing it as a **servant of our mission.**

Money makes a terrible master. but a powerful tool when led by wisdom and foresight.

SECTION 2. **Stewardship Before Strategy**

Before God teaches you **how** to multiply wealth, He teaches you **how** to carry it.

Strategy is essential, but stewardship comes first.

"You shall remember the Lord your God, for it is he who gives you power to get wealth..." — Deuteronomy 8:18 (NIV)

God gives the power, but stewardship determines whether you can handle it. Many believers ask for overflow but haven't mastered order.

They say:
- "God, bless my business"—but don't track expenses.
- "God, increase my finances"—but have no budget.
- "God, make me a lender"—but spend recklessly.

Stewardship Looks Like:
- Knowing what's coming in and what's going out
- Paying what's due, sowing what's instructed, saving what's wise
- Honoring God first, not last
- Building systems of trust and accountability

You don't need a million dollars to start stewarding like the Kingdom. Start with what's in your hand.

> *"He who is faithful with little will be faithful with much."* — Luke 16:10 (NIV)

Faithfulness is not about amount; it's about **attitude and alignment**.

If God can trust you with small decisions, He can trust you with enormous influence.

SECTION 3. What God Rewards with More

God doesn't reward hustle; He rewards **honor**.

When you align yourself with God's ways, you don't need to manipulate results. It's about stewardship, not striving.

What does God look for?

- **Obedience** – Are you following God's principles even when it stretches your faith?
- **Integrity** – Are you honest with money, even when no one's watching?
- **Generosity** – Are you willing to release when God says to sow?
- **Gratitude** – Do you thank Him in both plenty and lean seasons?
- **Wisdom** – Are you preparing for the future, not just reacting to the present?

God doesn't mind blessing your wallet. He wants to guard your worship.

The wise steward doesn't chase money; they **attract** it through alignment.

SECTION 4. Foresight Over Fear

Foresight is the ability to look ahead with wisdom, something every steward of Kingdom finances must develop.

> *"The prudent see danger and take refuge, but the simple keep going and pay the penalty."* — Proverbs 22:3

Fear reacts. Foresight prepares. The world system teaches panic and greed. The Kingdom teaches **prudence and peace**.

Foresight Doesn't Mean Hoarding—It Means Honoring

- Honoring God with your planning
- Honoring future opportunities through savings
- Honoring your family through margin and protection
- Honoring your calling through wise investments of time, money, and energy

Foresight, in the context of financial stewardship, is faith looking forward. It's not about being driven by the fear of lack, but about firmly believing that **God has more in store for us.**

There's a profound peace that comes from being prepared. You don't wait until the need arises to get ready. You prepare in peace before the pressure arrives.

Foresight isn't fear-driven—it's **future-ready.**

When it comes to seizing opportunities, the difference between the wise and the foolish isn't the presence of the opportunity but **the level of preparation.** Foresight is the key to being prepared for the right opportunities.

SECTION 5. Reflection Questions

1. How do I currently view money? as a tool, a threat, or a source?
2. Where in my finances am I faithful, and where am I neglecting stewardship?
3. What financial habit or system do I need to put in place this week?
4. How can I shift from fear-based financial decisions to foresight-led preparation?
5. Where do I need to invite God's wisdom into my money habits right now?

SECTION 6. Prayer Declaration

Father, I thank You for being my Source. Teach me to see money the way You do—not as a burden, but as a blessing to steward. I reject fear and embrace foresight. Make me a wise and faithful steward, not just in what I earn, but in how I honor You with it. Align my heart with Your priorities and let Your wisdom guide every decision I make. I trust You. I obey You, and I thank You for the overflow that comes through alignment. In Jesus' name, amen.

Chapter 7.2

Mastering Money Before It Masters You

Scripture Focus:
Proverbs 22:7, Matthew 6:24, Romans 13:8,
1 Timothy 6:6–10

Proverbs 22:7 (KJV) *7 The rich ruleth over the poor, and the borrower is servant to the lender.*

Matthew 6:24 (KJV) *24 No man can serve two masters: for either he will hate the one, and love the other; or else he will hold to the one, and despise the other. Ye cannot serve God and mammon.*

Romans 13:8 (KJV) *8 Owe no man any thing, but to love one another: for he that loveth another hath fulfilled the law.*

1 Timothy 6:6-10 (KJV) *6 But godliness with contentment is great gain. 7 For we brought nothing into this world, and it is certain we can carry nothing out. 8 And having food and raiment let us be therewith content. 9 But they that will be rich fall into temptation and a snare, and into many foolish and hurtful lusts, which drown men in destruction and perdition. 10 For the love of money is the root of all evil: which while some coveted after, they have erred from the faith, and pierced themselves through with many sorrows.*

INTRODUCTION. If You Don't Master It, It Will Master You

Money is an excellent servant, but a ruthless master.

Many people believe they control their money, but it controls them. Money is never neutral. It's always headed somewhere, being used for something, and influencing someone. It can be used to feed the hungry, clothe the naked, and heal the sick, or somebody can use it to exploit, oppress, and destroy. The question is, **are you in charge of it, or is it in charge of you?**

> *"The rich rule over the poor, and the borrower is slave to the lender."*
> — Proverbs 22:7 (NIV)

Solomon, the wisest man to ever live, didn't describe debt in terms of inconvenience. He called it **slavery.**

Jesus said, 'You cannot serve both God and mammon' (Matthew 6:24). This means that every financial decision is **a spiritual decision.** If money drives you, it will deceive you. But if you let God lead you, His principles will provide for you, giving you the confidence that you are on the right path.

In this world, money has influence. It affects decisions, relationships, and even access to resources. But in the Kingdom, if you serve another master other than **the Spirit of God,** it goes against your calling.

You are not just earning and spending. You are **either stewarding under God's authority or drifting under money's dominion** because money competes for lordship. It offers the same promises as God—security, identity, comfort, and power—but delivers counterfeit results and spiritual bondage.

The issue of money is more than a budgeting issue. It's a **lordship issue.** Jesus wasn't speaking to atheists or materialists; He was warning the people of God because mammon doesn't just want your attention; it wants your allegiance.

If you don't learn to **lead your money,** money will lead you. And when money leads, you end up chasing peace, purpose, and identity in places that cannot fulfill you.

This chapter is not about financial advice; it's about **spiritual alignment.** We're going to expose the subtle power of money, confront the lies we've believed, and build a foundation where wisdom, freedom, and foresight can thrive.

Whether you're drowning in debt, climbing in income, or just trying to make ends meet, this is your invitation to **take authority,** walk in clarity, and live like a steward who's already won the war over wealth. You have the power to take control of your finances and live a life aligned with your spiritual values.

SECTION 1. The Spiritual Battle Over Your Wallet

"No one can serve two masters... You cannot serve both God and money." — Matthew 6:24 (NIV)

Let that verse sink in. You cannot. Not "shouldn't," not "try not to," but **cannot**.

Jesus didn't make a suggestion; He revealed a spiritual law. Money is not just physical; it's spiritual. It has presence, pressure, and power. If left unchallenged, it will shape how you live, what you love, and who you trust.

Money's Competing Promises

The spirit of mammon (a demonic spirit assigned to money that Jesus named explicitly) mimics the role of God by offering:
- **Security** – "If you have enough, you'll never worry."
- **Identity** – "Your worth is in your wealth."
- **Power** – "People will respect you if you have it."
- **Freedom** – "You can do whatever you want when you're rich."
- **Peace** – "Money will fix your stress."
- **Protection** – "Savings will shield you from harm."

But these are cunning deceptions disguised as logic. We've all heard these seductive whispers. And most of us have followed them at some point, sometimes without realizing it.

Money promises what only God can provide and then quietly demands worship in return.

Jesus didn't compare money to sin, pride, or selfishness. He compared it directly to **God**. That should terrify us and awaken us.

The Subtle Signs of a Mastered Life

You might not think money is running your life, but here are some signs:
- You **obsess over financial safety** more than spiritual obedience
- You **choose jobs** based on pay, not purpose
- You **worry about giving** because "you might need it."

- You **fear tithing** because your budget feels tight
- You **measure success** by your income, not your impact
- You **compare your provision** to someone else's pace

The truth? Money doesn't have to be your idol to master you—it only needs to control your decisions.

But here's the breakthrough:

When you submit your money to God, it loses its power over you. When it becomes a tool instead of a god, it becomes a **weapon for the Kingdom.**

This battle is real. But it's one you can win. Let's go deeper.

SECTION 2. Freedom from Debt and the Pressure to Perform

"Let no debt remain outstanding, except the continuing debt to love one another..." — Romans 13:8 (NIV)

Debt isn't just a math problem; it's a mindset trap. It keeps you locked into a cycle of pressure, fear, and regret. And in a culture that celebrates overspending and instant gratification, debt often disguises itself as **normal.**

But what's common isn't always the Kingdom.

The Reality of Debt in the Church

God's people are to lend and not borrow (Deuteronomy 28:12), yet statistics show that the average Christian household carries thousands of dollars in consumer debt.

Why?

Because we believe that the only way to live well is to **live beyond our means.**

We finance what we can't afford, justifying it with phrases like:
- "It's just temporary."
- "Everyone has debt."
- "I'll pay it off later."
- "It's a good kind of debt."

But over time, those small compromises compound, and soon, your income isn't funding your vision; it's servicing your past.

The High Cost of Borrowed Peace

Debt doesn't just cost money, it costs:
- **Sleep** – from anxiety about payments
- **Joy** – from shame over poor choices
- **Flexibility** – to move or serve when God calls
- **Generosity** – because your giving is a part of your service

You can't give what belongs to the lender. You can't build when you're busy bailing out your budget.

And worst of all, debt creates **a spirit of survival.** It makes you think small, dream less often, and stay stagnant.

But God's desire is freedom, not pressure.

"It is for freedom that Christ has set us free..." — Galatians 5:1 (NIV)

You were not born again to live in financial chains. Your calling is to live open-handed, purpose-driven, and free.

Breaking Free: The Spiritual Side of Debt

Freedom begins with repentance, not just from lousy spending but from misplaced trust.

Ask yourself:
- Have I been trusting in credit instead of Christ?
- Have I bought things to feel better about myself?
- Have I ignored God's voice in financial decisions?

Then, move into action:
- **Face your reality** – List every debt. Pray over each one.
- **Budget with integrity** – Every dollar gets an assignment.
- **Start the snowball** – Pay off all debt, from the smallest to the largest, with focus.
- **Honor God first** – Even in debt, tithe in faith.
- **Ask for a supernatural strategy** – God may lead you to sell, shift, or surrender something.

You don't need shame. You need a strategy. God is ready to lead you out of financial Egypt into a land of abundance.

SECTION 3. **Contentment Is a Weapon**

> *"But godliness with contentment is great gain."* — 1 Timothy 6:6 (NIV)

Most people think contentment is the **opposite of ambition**. But in the Kingdom, contentment is not complacency; it's **confidence** in the sufficiency of God.

You don't need more to be more. You don't need later to live now.
Contentment is a spiritual weapon because it allows you to:
- Stop comparing and start stewarding
- Say "no" to pressure and "yes" to peace
- Make decisions from faith, not fear
- Delay gratification without losing identity
- Save, invest, and give without resentment

The Culture of More

The world is allergic to contentment. The design of every ad, app, and algorithm is to make you feel behind, like you're missing something.
- New car? You need an upgrade.
- New house? You need more space.
- New phone? It's already old.
- New blessing? It's time to post it.

However, Scripture reveals that contentment is **a learned**, not innate, quality.

> *"I have learned the secret of being content in any and every situation..."* — Philippians 4:12 (NIV)

Paul wrote those words from a prison cell. Not a palace. Not after a bonus check. Not after a big win.

In chains, he found peace because contentment doesn't come from your **circumstance**; it comes from your **conviction**.

The Internal Shift

When you're content:
- You no longer need to prove yourself through purchases

- You stop measuring your success by someone else's season
- You make more well-thought-out, longer-term financial decisions
- You see your current income as a seed, not a ceiling
- You carry peace even while waiting for a promotion

When you're discontent:
- You overspend to impress
- You delay generosity because "it's not enough."
- You make financial moves that you later regret
- You chase success without ever feeling satisfied

Contentment silences the voice of mammon and re-centers your heart around the faithfulness of God.

It's not about settling. It's about **gaining a clear, unwavering perspective on what truly matters.**

You can be grateful for today while preparing for tomorrow. Striking a balance between contentment and continued growth while still expecting and working towards more is the sweet spot of spiritual and financial stewardship.

SECTION 4. Habits of a Financially Free Steward

Financial freedom isn't about how much you make; it's about how much you **master.** Mastery comes from **habits**, not dreams, wishes, or hype.

Jesus said that the faithful steward is the one who **manages well** (Luke 16:10). Therefore, the goal is greater **faithfulness.**

Six Habits that Keep You in Authority

1. **Tithing with Joy**
   Tithing isn't about money; it's about mastery. It's a declaration of trust saying, *"God, I trust You with the first, and I believe You'll bless the rest."*
   Faithful stewards don't tithe last or out of leftovers; they tithe first, in **honor and obedience.** I always say, "Tithing is not just 10% of your increase; it's the first 10% of your increase."

2. **Tracking Every Dollar**
   You can't lead what you don't measure. Stewards know what's coming in, what's going out, and where it's going.
   It's not about restriction as much as it is about **revelation.** Budgeting helps you determine if your lifestyle aligns with your assignment.

3. **Living Below Your Means**
   Wealthy or not, wise stewards create margin. They don't spend everything they make. They leave room for giving, saving, and responding to God's voice as well as unexpected needs.
   Margin creates **peace and power.**

4. **Saving with Foresight**
   Savings is not a lack of faith; it's a fruit of wisdom. You're not hoarding; you're preparing.
   Joseph didn't just interpret Pharaoh's dream; he built systems of **supply and survival.** God honored that foresight.

5. **Giving When Prompted**
   Free stewards listen. They're sensitive to the Holy Spirit and are quick to sow.
   Giving isn't just an act of obedience; it's a demonstration of your freedom. It stretches you, proves your freedom, and activates God's provision.

6. **Praying Over Your Finances**
   Wise stewards don't just calculate; they **consecrate.**
   Every budget meeting is a prayer meeting. Every financial decision is an altar. Wise stewards seek wisdom, bind fear, and release blessings over their homes.
   Habits aren't glamorous. But they lead to freedom, and freedom leads to fruit.

SECTION 5. Reflection Questions

1. Where have I allowed money to master my decisions, emotions, or priorities?
2. What financial habits need breaking, and which ones need building up?
3. Do I give, save, and spend reactively or with foresight?

4. Am I truly content in this season, or restless to prove something?
5. What is one financial obedience step God is asking me to take this week?

SECTION 6. Prayer Declaration

Father, I declare that money is not my master. I am led by Your Spirit, grounded in Your Word, and governed by Your wisdom. I break every agreement with fear, greed, and the pressure to perform. I choose peace over pressure, purpose over performance, and contentment over comparison. I tithe in joy, give in faith, save with foresight, and steward with integrity. I surrender every dollar I receive. Cause my money to be sanctified and assigned. I am a steward of the Kingdom, and I walk in financial freedom. In Jesus' name, amen.

Chapter 7.3

Funding Vision with Kingdom Foresight

Scripture Focus:
Habakkuk 2:2–3, Proverbs 21:20, Luke 14:28–30, 2 Corinthians 9:10–11

Habakkuk 2:2-3 (KJV) *2 And the LORD answered me, and said, Write the vision, and make it plain upon tables, that he may run that readeth it. 3 For the vision is yet for an appointed time, but at the end it shall speak, and not lie: though it tarry, wait for it; because it will surely come, it will not tarry.*

Proverbs 21:20 (KJV) *20 There is treasure to be desired and oil in the dwelling of the wise; but a foolish man spendeth it up.*

Luke 14:28-30 (KJV) *28 For which of you, intending to build a tower, sitteth not down first, and counteth the cost, whether he have sufficient to finish it? 29 Lest haply, after he hath laid the foundation, and is not able to finish it, all that behold it begin to mock him, 30 Saying, This man began to build, and was not able to finish.*

2 Corinthians 9:10-11 (KJV) *10 Now he that ministereth seed to the sower both minister bread for your food, and multiply your seed sown, and increase the fruits of your righteousness;) 11 Being enriched in every thing to all bountifulness, which causeth through us thanksgiving to God.*

INTRODUCTION. Provision Doesn't Chase Wishes

Provision follows vision, not emotion, not ambition, not need, but vision.

One of the most overlooked stewardship principles in the Bible is that God funds what He assigns. This means if your vision is truly God-given, you have not only the Kingdom's backing but also access to the Kingdom's resources. However, access requires stewardship. It demands discipline, the kind that empowers you to make wise decisions and take control of your financial journey. It demands foresight, the ability to see beyond the present and plan for the future. You don't receive resources just because you're hopeful; you receive and retain resources when you're faithful.

As Habakkuk declared:

> *"Write the vision and make it plain on tablets, so that he may run who reads it. For still the vision awaits its appointed time; it hastens to the end*—it will not lie. If it seems slow, wait for it; it will surely come; it will not delay." — Habakkuk 2:2–3 (ESV)

The command to write the vision isn't just about clarity; it's about preparation. A written vision serves as your guide and compass on the financial journey. It guides practical decisions, helping you build structures and direct resources with intention. It allows you to live with purpose, making decisions that align with your vision rather than reacting to life haphazardly.

When we lack vision, we waste provisions. We spend emotionally instead of prophetically, which means spending in alignment with God's plan and purpose. We make decisions based on fear, not faith. We chase open doors without discerning divine direction. But when we embrace foresight, our finances shift from frustration to fuel.

This chapter will equip you to:
- Turn your vision into a working financial strategy
- Build storehouses and financial structures that honor God
- Move from spontaneous giving to Spirit-led investing
- Walk in Kingdom wisdom that multiplies your provision over time

Because in the Kingdom, wealth without vision is like rain without a vessel—it evaporates before it can irrigate your assignment.

SECTION 1. The Blueprint – Vision Is the First Budget

"Suppose one of you wants to build a tower. Won't you first sit down and estimate the cost to see if you have enough money to complete it?" — Luke 14:28 (NIV)

Jesus wasn't just talking about construction. He was revealing a spiritual principle: you cannot steward what you haven't structured.

When most people think about budgets, they think about numbers, spreadsheets, apps, or even restrictions. But in the Kingdom, your first budget isn't financial—it's prophetic. It begins with a vision.

Your vision determines your yes and your no. For instance, if your vision is to be debt-free, you will say no to unnecessary expenses and yes to saving and investing. It defines your financial boundaries and opportunities. It helps you identify what to pursue and what to postpone.

Without vision:
- Every opportunity seems like an obligation
- You chase scattered investments and commitments
- You confuse motion with momentum and movement with mission
- You say yes to people and projects that drain your assignment

However, with a clear vision, your finances become assignment-driven. They are not tossed around by crisis or cultural pressure but are aimed like arrows toward destiny.

SECTION 2. Turning Vision into a Financial Plan

1. **Write the Vision in Detail**
   Vague visions kill discipline. Don't just say, "I want to start a ministry" or "I want to open a business." Get specific: What kind? What is the cost? What are the timelines? Who are the people it serves? Write the details as if preparing blueprints for construction.

2. **Break the Vision into Phases**
   Large visions can be overwhelming and lead to unnecessary stress. Instead of trying to accomplish everything at once, break your

vision into manageable 90-day goals. These short-term milestones will help you maintain focus and manage your budget effectively.

3. **Forecast Resources Required**
   What money, people, tools, training, and systems will you need in the next quarter? Next year? Begin with what is in your hand. Remember how God asked Moses, "What is that in your hand?"

4. **Build Around Purpose, Not Pressure**
   Let purpose lead your priorities. If you let pressure determine your spending, your vision will become a casualty of your bills—budget by calling, not crisis.

5. **Pray Over the Budget, Not Just the Blessing**
   Too many believers pray for overflow without praying for order. If your financial structure can't handle the increase, God, in His mercy, may withhold it until you mature.

6. **Review and Adjust Every 30 Days**
   Vision must remain dynamic. Check your progress. Revisit your numbers. Adjust timelines based on results, not just dreams. **God often gives vision in layers.**

7. **Communicate the Vision**
   Share the vision with key stakeholders such as mentors, intercessors, family members, or team members, who can help hold you accountable. Vision thrives in clarity, but it multiplies in community.

8. **Make Room for Divine Disruption**
   Foresight also includes flexibility. When God redirects, don't resist. Wise stewards balance structure with surrender.

When you define the vision, provision gets defined. If you don't define the assignment, money will define it for you, and often, it will lead you into detours.

SECTION 3. Build the Storehouse Before the Storm

"The wise store up choice food and olive oil, but fools gulp theirs down." — Proverbs 21:20 (NIV)

One of the most Kingdom-defining disciplines is preparation. And one of the most overlooked financial disciplines is building a storehouse.

In ancient times, a storehouse was a literal structure—a barn, a cellar, or a vault. Its purpose was to preserve and protect surplus. Today, the storehouse refers to any intentional system that captures overflow and redirects it toward the Kingdom's purpose.

God doesn't bless chaos. He blesses preparation:

"The Lord will command the blessing on your barns and in all that you undertake." — Deuteronomy 28:8 (ESV)

Notice the wording: God commands the blessing on your barns. Not your emotions, not your intentions, your barns, or your systems.

Modern Storehouses May Include:
- A savings account for emergencies or business opportunities
- An investment fund for retirement or future growth
- A giving account set aside for sowing and missions
- A legal entity to structure generational wealth
- A financial system that tracks income and expenses with purpose
- A donor-advised fund for legacy giving
- A home office or physical space dedicated to business or ministry

Why You Must Build a Storehouse

1. **Vision Without Structure Leaks**
   If you don't have a place for the increase to flow, it will be absorbed by reactionary spending. **God is not wasteful—He is purposeful.** He won't pour where there is no plan.

2. **Blessing Requires Boundaries**
   God filled the temple *after* it was prepared (1 Kings 8:10-11). He filled the jars *after* they were gathered (2 Kings 4:2-6). When you build structure, you invite blessings.

3. **Harvest Requires Storage**
   Joseph saved grain not out of fear but foresight. Egypt fed nations during the famine because Joseph had a storehouse system. His wisdom preserved not just a country but a covenant.

4. **Surplus is a Stewardship Test**
   Most people cry out to God in times of need but forget Him in times of plenty. Storehouses keep you humble, disciplined, and future-focused.

5. **Preparedness Attracts Opportunity**
Investors, donors, and partners are drawn to prepared people. Structure signals stewardship. Your readiness can unlock resources from unexpected places.

SECTION 4. **Build Before the Storm**

We don't build an ark when it starts raining. We don't save when the emergency hits. We don't plan for expansion once we're overwhelmed.

Kingdom stewardship is proactive. When God says, "Prepare," don't wait for proof. Obey now. That's how Noah built the ark (Genesis 6:11-22). That's how Joseph saved the fifth part (Genesis 41:34 and 47:24-26). That's how wise believers thrive.

SECTION 5. **Sowing into Vision with Foresight**

> *"Now he who supplies seed to the Sower and bread for food will also supply and increase your store of seed and will enlarge the harvest of your righteousness."* — 2 Corinthians 9:10 (NIV)

One of the most significant marks of maturity is the ability to recognize what to consume and what to sow. Immature stewards eat what they should plant. They turn seeds for harvest into snacks, delaying their destiny.

In the Kingdom, not all provisions are for spending. Some are for sowing, some are for saving, and some are for sending. Foresight helps you discern the difference.

Don't Just Give—Invest in Destiny

God is not just looking for emotional givers. He's raising strategic stewards. Spirit-led giving is about accuracy, not applause. It flows from alignment, not anxiety.

Emotional Giving	Strategic Sowing
Impulsive	Intentional
Motivated by pressure	Motivated by prayer
Driven by emotion	Driven by assignment
Focused on immediate relief	Focused on eternal reward

Your giving should extend your calling. Don't scatter seeds out of guilt. Sow with intention. Identify ministries, movements, missionaries, and leaders that align with your mandate.

Give Like a Farmer, not a Gambler

Farmers don't toss seeds randomly. They sow strategically:
- In the right season
- On fertile ground
- With a long-term harvest in mind

That means you should:
- Schedule regular giving (monthly, quarterly)
- Set aside a portion for spontaneous Spirit-led giving
- Measure giving by obedience, not just amount
- Track harvests tied to your seed so you can give thanks and stay faithful

Aligning with the Kingdom's Vision

When you give according to God's instruction, your seed carries a supernatural assignment. Provision multiplies, doors open, and favor increases because God breathes on what aligns with His purpose.

Strategic sowing doesn't just bless the receiver—it transforms the giver. It cultivates faith, clarity, and consistent breakthroughs.

Stories of Foresight in Giving

- A businesswoman sowed a year's worth of tithe in advance toward a mission she hadn't yet launched. Six months later, a donor came and funded the entire launch.

- A family gave away their second car and, within 90 days, were gifted a new one, valued twice as much.
- A small church gave generously to another local ministry. Within a year, their building project received miraculous funding.

These are not formulas—they're fruit. When you give with foresight, you step into partnership with God's purpose.

Remember: God *supplies seed to sowers* (2 Corinthians 9:10), not to consumers. This means that God entrusts resources to those who are willing to invest them wisely and for His purposes. If you want more seed, become a faithful planter.

SECTION 6. Reflection Questions:

1. What has God called me to build or release in this season?
2. Do I have a clear financial plan to fund the vision, or am I reacting without a roadmap?
3. Where can I start preparing a "storehouse" for future assignments or increases?
4. Do I give based on prayer, purpose, and foresight, or pressure and emotion?
5. What is one habit I can implement this week to steward vision with foresight?
6. Who can I ask to hold me accountable for my financial stewardship?
7. What does faithfulness look like in this season of resource?

SECTION 7. Prayer Declaration

Father, thank You for the vision You've placed in my heart. I receive it with both faith and responsibility. Teach me to walk in foresight, not just fervor. Give me wisdom to plan, discipline to prepare, and grace to steward. I declare that every dollar I receive will serve a Kingdom purpose. I will not waste the increase but channel it toward the assignment. I call forth storehouses, strategies, and sustained provision. I will write the vision, count the cost, and walk with wisdom. In Jesus' name, amen.

Book Summary

Throughout this journey, we have uncovered seven transformational keys that unlock a life of Kingdom stewardship. Each chapter has invited you to see your life not as random or reactive, but as a sacred assignment. You have a calling to manage what matters, to live with vision, to act with wisdom, and to multiply what Heaven has entrusted into your hands.

You've seen that stewardship is not limited to finances—it extends to your thoughts, your time, your voice, your work, and your worship. It touches every corner of your calling. Every part of your life is sacred real estate. And God is looking for faithful tenants who will cultivate, grow, and glorify Him with what He's entrusted to them.

Here's what you've mastered:
- You now **see** more clearly—vision fuels purpose
- You **think** with wisdom—truth renews your mind
- You **speak** with power—words shape destiny
- You **work** with excellence—effort honors the Master
- You **express** gratitude—thankfulness multiplies joy
- You **manage time** with prudence—seasons reveal strategy
- You **handle money** with foresight—resources fuel vision

Each key you've learned is a tool, and each tool requires action. The fruit of this book isn't in the pages read but in **the lives transformed.**

"It is required in stewards that one be found faithful." — 1 Corinthians 4:2

But faithfulness is only the beginning. God desires that you become not just a **faithful steward** but a **fruitful one**—a builder, a multiplier, a trusted vessel who brings forth 30, 60, and 100-fold.

You are that steward.

As you now move into the bonus journal, don't simply review the content. Let the Holy Spirit renew your commitments. Let vision be refreshed. Let action be activated.

Because your story isn't finished.

You've been entrusted with vision.

You've been equipped with wisdom.

Now, it's time to **build what God has shown you.**

Bonus Journal

7 Stewardship Keys That Lead to Overflow

Stewardship Keys Self-Assessment

Key 1 – Vision: What You See

- Am I dreaming with God or limited by fear?
- What has God shown me that I need to write down and act on?
- How do I protect my imagination from distraction and distortion?

Key 2 – Knowledge: What You Think

- What am I currently feeding my mind with?
- Where do I need a greater understanding to walk in wisdom?
- Am I willing to unlearn what culture taught me and relearn what the Word says?

Key 3 – Confession: What You Say

- Are my words aligned with what I believe—or what I fear?
- What declarations do I need to speak over my life daily?
- How have my words built or broken momentum this week?

Key 4 – Work & Wisdom: What You Do

- Am I showing up with excellence and diligence?
- What systems or habits would multiply my current effectiveness?
- Where am I working harder than I'm working wiser?

Key 5 – Gratitude: What You Express

- Have I paused to thank God in this season?
- Where have I complained instead of honored?
- What can I intentionally celebrate today?

Key 6 – Prudence: What You Do with Time

- Am I wasting, spending, or investing my time?
- What season am I in—and what does it require of me?
- Where do I need to say no to protect what matters most?

Key 7 – Foresight: What You Do with Money

- Is my money serving my mission—or sabotaging it?
- Do I have a written financial plan that reflects my values and vision?
- Where is God calling me to sow, store, or scale?

Prayer Declarations by Key

Key 1 – Vision: *Father, open my eyes to see what You see. I reject fear and receive prophetic clarity. I will write the vision and run with it.*

Key 2 – Knowledge: *God, I pursue wisdom and understanding. I will meditate on Your truth day and night. I think like Heaven.*

Key 3 – Confession: *My words are weapons. I speak life. I declare Your promises. My mouth agrees with my mission.*

Key 4 – Work & Wisdom: *I am diligent, disciplined, and Spirit-led. I build with excellence. My hands are blessed to prosper.*

Key 5 – Gratitude: *I thank You, Lord, for all You've done and all You're doing. I live from joy, not jealousy. I honor the present.*

Key 6 – Prudence (Time): *Teach me to number my days. I move in rhythm with Heaven. I say yes with clarity and no with peace.*

Key 7 – Foresight (Money): *Provision follows vision. I steward finances with purpose. I am not mastered by money—I master it for Your glory. In Jesus' Name, Amen.*

Weekly Stewardship Tracker

Stewardship Area	Focus This Week	Action Step	Fruit Seen
Vision			
Knowledge			
Confession			
Work & Wisdom			
Gratitude			
Time			
Money			

Print and use this each week to reflect, track progress, and stay aligned.

Activation Page

My Stewardship Commitment

I, _____, commit to steward my life with wisdom, faith, and foresight. I will pursue vision, seek understanding, speak truth, work with diligence, express gratitude, manage time intentionally, and honor God with my finances.

Signed: _____ Date: _____

Epilogue

A Golden Opportunity

Choosing to receive Jesus Christ as your Lord and Savior is the most important decision you'll ever make!

Romans 10:9-10, 13 (NKJV) 9 that if you confess with your mouth the Lord Jesus and believe in your heart that God has raised Him from the dead, you will be saved. 10 For with the heart one believes unto righteousness, and with the mouth confession is made unto salvation. 13 For "whoever calls on the name of the LORD shall be saved.

By His grace, God has already done everything to provide salvation. Your part is to believe and receive.

Pray out loud, "Dear Lord, I come to You now, just as I am. You know my life. You know how I've lived. Forgive me, Lord. I repent of my sins. I believe Jesus Christ is the Son of God. He died for my sins, and on the third day, God raised Him from the dead. Lord Jesus, I ask You to come into my heart. Live Your life in me and through me from now on. From this day forward, I belong to You. Lord, I ask that you please fill me with Your Holy Spirit. In the Name of Jesus, Amen."

The very moment you commit your life to Jesus Christ; the truth of His Word instantly comes to pass in your spirit.

If you prayed that prayer and believed it in your heart, a miracle has just taken place in your life, and there's a brand-new you!

Don't hesitate to get in touch with us and let us know that you've prayed to receive Jesus as your Lord and Savior. We want to rejoice with you and help you understand more fully what has taken place in your life. We have information that we would like to share with you. Please visit www.JasonHaleMinistries.org, complete the contact form, and expect to receive an email from us containing the next steps to help you understand and grow in your new relationship with the Lord.

Welcome to the Kingdom of Almighty God!

About the Author

For over 28 years, God's Servant, Jason Hale has dedicated himself to helping people excel in every area of their lives. His ministry, speaking engagements, workshops, and newly released book all work in conjunction with this deeply rooted passion. Through the power of storytelling and the application of Biblical principles, Jason teaches ministers, churches, corporate leaders, laypeople, organizations, and sales teams how to draw near to God and excel supernaturally at the same time.

Jason has six children and a fourth grandchild on the way at the time of this publication. He has been a U.S. Army veteran since 1990, an Ordained Minister since 1997, and an entrepreneur since 1998.

www.ingramcontent.com/pod-product-compliance
Lightning Source LLC
Chambersburg PA
CBHW070647160426
43194CB00009B/1616